Sweet Days and Roses

Sweet Days and Roses

AN ANTHOLOGY OF GARDEN WRITING

RYLAND
PETERS
& SMALL
LONDON NEW YORK

EDITED AND WITH COMMENTARIES BY LESLIE GEDDES-BROWN

DESIGNER *Emilie Ekström*
SENIOR EDITOR *Henrietta Heald*
PICTURE RESEARCH *Emily Westlake*
PRODUCTION *Patricia Harrington*
ART DIRECTOR *Gabriella Le Grazie*
PUBLISHING DIRECTOR *Alison Starling*

PROOFREADER *Alison Bravington*

This collection first published in
the United Kingdom in 2003 by
Ryland Peters & Small

Kirkman House
12–14 Whitfield Street
London WIT 2RP
www.rylandpeters.com
10 9 8 7 6 5 4 3 2 1

Introduction, selection and commentaries text
copyright © Leslie Geddes-Brown 2003
For other text copyright, see pages 156–57
Photograph on page 140 copyright © Steve Painter
Photographs on pages 51 and 155 copyright
© Jonathan Buckley
Line drawings reproduced from *Plants & Flowers*
courtesy of Dover Publications, Inc., New York.
All other photographs, illustrations and design
copyright © Ryland Peters & Small 2003

ISBN 1 84172 407 6

A CIP record for this book is available from
the British Library.

Printed and bound in China.

Contents

Introduction 6

Chapter One Garden Glory 8

Chapter Two Designs and Schemes 38

Chapter Three Plant Passions 74

Chapter Four The Gardeners 120

Acknowledgments 156

Picture credits 158

Index of authors 160

Introduction

I am a voracious reader – the telephone book, backs of shampoo labels – and regard the anthology as a life-saver. Somerset Maugham used to cart a sackful of books on his extensive voyages. The anthology is the modern traveller's version.

This is one in a long string of garden anthologies but, since each comes with the imprint of its editor, each is different. I have tried to pick excerpts that are not primarily intended for serious gardeners (a doughty bunch) in that some are comical, some highly prejudiced and some show, in detail, the deep eccentricities of gardeners. Other pieces are aimed at turning those who hate the idea of lifting a spade into fanatic gardeners.

When I first started to snip and deadhead (I've never been much of a spade-wielder myself) and, more enjoyably still, to buy new plants, I was driven on by the inspiring, poetic – and short – pieces written by Vita Sackville-West, who could tempt you into buying a dandelion, such was her passionate advocacy. The same goes for Christopher Lloyd, lyrical and dogmatic by turns.

Other selections contain ideas that strike me as highly original, such as Helen Dillon's yellow garden. Until I read her piece, I hated the very thought of such a garden. Now I'm converted.

I've enjoyed every minute of making this book, especially since I have met many of the writers or visited their creations. I hope readers – on trains, as house guests, filling an empty half-hour, looking for garden inspiration – will have as much fun as I did.

I

Garden Glory

Garden writers are not always gardeners – some survive with no more than a roof terrace – but you don't have to be a footballer to write about football. The best garden writing combines observation – of plant partners and subtle design – with inspiration. Gardeners often work instinctively and it may take outsiders to spot, and describe, beauty when they find it.

When I met Mirabel Osler, she was already an established garden writer and A Gentle Plea for Chaos *(1989) had become a hit. She had recently moved to a town house in Ludlow with a small garden. With characteristic verve, she had already planned it and planted it. It was full of ideas that inspired gardeners after her: she refused to have a lawn, insisting on great deep beds mulched with dark wood chippings, and her garden was full of small rooms, each with its own furniture painted to match both the outhouses and the plants. 'Why Garden?' appeared in an early issue of* Hortus *magazine.*

Why garden?

I think I may know. The reason creeps up on you slowly. Like a childhood memory of gardens its origins may begin with a mild hankering, a non-thinking conformity, or just an erosion of your peace of mind by writers and photographers. Whichever way you succumbed there is no going back. Gardens are as compulsive as hunger and warmth.

Each gardener must have begun from a different incentive and perhaps the most common reason is merely physical – just by having a piece of land, a space, an area of debris or a thicket of weeds outside the window. And yet it isn't that simple. Look at a row of back gardens in a city and you see a variety of responses. Some are cultivated, some are totally neglected. So where is the germ? Where is the seed which lies dormant in some of us and doesn't even exist in others?

For years my mind was closed to gardening. I wanted none of it. Children and animals had held us down for so many years it seemed sense that once through them, then there would be freedom. And when we were living in Greece, when we had sea, mountains and wild flowers to offer, too many friends being invited to stay had said, 'We can't both come – the garden can't be left.' Or 'I couldn't possibly be away then, the day lilies are at their best.' The what?

Yet I can almost remember a day when sitting in a chair on a warm Mediterranean spring noon, when the asphodels … were so prolific around us, the view at eye level was a pinkish glaucoma. Sitting in total idleness, slack and vacant, my hand dangled on the damp earth and I suddenly thought if I weren't careful my fingers would take root in such fecund ground. From that moment something shifted. A small grain of impulsion, curiosity or awareness – a small Why Not? germinated.

Why do gardeners garden? What is the attraction? Look around and the answer is so obvious that supposedly no one has asked the question. The whole of England flourishes with gardens and it happens from something more than boredom or convention; it is subtler than the mere appreciation of flowers. The scope for creativeness is infinite. With each of us our eyes are different; our intake of colours so varied; our response and alignment so individual. Give several people the same space and dimensions to cultivate and think what a variety of solutions you would end up with. Not just because of the part of the country you live in or the type of soil or the altitude you may have, of course these count, but gardens are comprised of so much more than flowers, shrubs and trees.

There is another element. Forceful and invisible; it is as if a garden once started by you with care and forethought becomes a growing entity well outside your own life. Gardens grow. They go on growing; they may even take over. They do. In fact in the end you can have a love-hate feeling for this great yeasty creature – this thing that keeps 'working'.

It is then that what each of us decides to do with this culture will make the contrast of gardens we see everywhere. It depends on how restrictively we control and contain that ferment. How much we allow it to spread or alternatively restrain its momentum; how we see colours, arrange shapes or understand the inherent value of each plant. And something else too. So much depends on how ruthless we are with failure. We each at one time or another have walked round our garden looking at a grossly overgrown shrub or an overpowering patch of saxifrage and said, 'Oh I must do something about that!', when obviously we haven't and won't. A coward lives with his mistakes – hoping for a change of attitude towards it next year or that by planting something nearby the mistake will be filtered. The brave man does it with a sword. And it is then that you discover one of the many unexpected pleasures of gardening – the relief when finally with decision and courage you do remove that hideous forsythia you had hoped you would come to love.

Pleasures? Oh, yes, for gardeners there are many. Not only achievement, which is obvious and surely will happen some time to even the most acid-fingered of us. But unexpected pleasures. For instance, one of mine is to go round the garden untwining an uncompliant clematis scrambling into the wrong rose. With infinite patience I must delicately unpick a tendril that holds the stem with the tenacity of a baby's finger. To make it grow the way I want and not in the arbitrary direction the wind has taken it requires the precision of unpicking Victorian hem-stitching. That's a pleasure I had not imagined.

But there is the other side too. That burgeoning flora outside the window is a creature you cannot shut out, even when you are dead-beat in the summer days when you cannot possibly draw the curtain against all that flowers. There it is, pulling at you, calling, needing you. Waiting to be noticed or waiting for water – either way it gets you. And although it can be calming to consider the liquid manure it takes to make a peach – it is not necessarily something you want crammed down your throat every time you turn towards the light.

Why garden? Some of us know. For so many reasons; once begun, the reasons proliferate. We, for instance, grow shrub roses which are often criticized for their short flowering season and yet we don't expect daffodils to reappear in summer or buddleias to bloom for Easter. Imagine the tedium if roses bloomed all the year – what anticipation we would miss looking at the black sticks in winter which we know, but hardly believe, contain next summer's garden. And it is that swing of season that partly answers the question. The bleak melancholy of a winter garden full of debris not tidied up in time before the frost and snow arrive, the sight of that desolation and bareness, that is the reason; to be confounded one day when there really will be summer again, when we will have to believe our eyes.

So roses for many of us are certainly responsible. They do answer the question – Why Garden? There is 'Belle de Crécy' whose strange colour forms contusions on the ageing petals;

or 'Mme Hardy' with her surprising viridian eye; 'Ricardii' whose hundreds of single blossoms are as transitory as dew; and 'Souvenir de la Malmaison' with its quartered delicacy. But there is a further intrinsic reason for gardening – not just for the plants themselves which are forever carrying us along – but because a garden is always on the move. You have never, never arrived. Next year will be different from this one – nothing will be concluded, nothing will be static, however hard we have tried, and we all at some time have wanted to do this, to hold back the growth just as it is. To keep the perfect days so that what we have laboured over and nourished, petted and protected, can be held at its zenith; when everything somehow has come off right and the colour, blooming and survival have all happened at once – then how badly we would like to hold it just so. Just to be able to prevent those petals from opening further; to stop the sun or rain from destroying such perfection. The moments are rare enough indeed, but what joy it would be to be able to petrify the whole fulfilment for just a few days more. It never happens. On, on, that uncontrollable force is pushing us so that inevitably we are already planning for this moment to happen again next year. Only then, naturally, it will be even more perfect. And there is the flaw. What gardener isn't of two minds? Even as you are sighing with satisfaction with what you have at last pulled off after three, five or ten years of endeavour – the other ambitious mind is already making greedy notes for what must be done next year.

It's not like that with cooking! You cook a meal; either it is a success or it is all right; or uneatable. But at the time, in the proper Zen mentality, you are concentrating on making that meal. But not a gardener. That split mind; those compelling lists. Those bullying little notes to yourself for even further perfection. All to be faced again in a year's time.

But wait, this is the very essence of gardening. This is the very incentive that keeps us going; the implicit fact that a garden is always on the move keeps up our pace. It is not us forcing it onwards, but long ago, unnoticed, this onus shifted and now – a garden started – it is the garden forcing us. We are indeed possessed. No wonder non-gardeners sometimes stand aghast and ask 'Why garden?'

Mirabel Osler, 'Why Garden?', Hortus, 1988

Actually, I don't agree with her about cooking. Just like gardening, there's always the vision of a better daube, a stickier roast pork or a more strongly garlicked aioli lurking in the future. Cooks, like gardeners, make notes and criticisms, and taste (rather than visualize) the perfect chunk of roast cod or sorrel omelette … next week, next year.

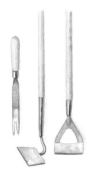

Virtue

Sweet day, so cool, so calm, so bright!
The bridal of the earth and sky –
The dew shall weep thy fall to-night;
For thou must die.

Sweet rose, whose hue angry and brave
Bids the rash gazer wipe his eye,
Thy root is ever in its grave,
And thou must die.

Sweet spring, full of sweet days and roses,
A box where sweets compacted lie,
My music shows ye have your closes,
And all must die.

Only a sweet and virtuous soul,
Like season'd timber, never gives;
But though the whole world turn to coal,
Then chiefly lives.

George Herbert (1593–1633)

The National Gardens Scheme of England and Wales, which recently had its 75th anniversary, is the biggest and best scheme of its kind in the world. Not only does it give money to charity and great pleasure to gardeners, allowing them opportunities to share their successes with others, it also inspires tyros and experts alike – as Anne Scott-James explains in a letter to her daughter.

Garden open today

Dearest C,

Now that the 'garden open' season has begun, we might try to visit a famous garden now and again on a Saturday or Sunday. These trips do open the eyes …

Garden visiting is now as popular a national pastime as football but without the danger of yobboes and riots. Personally I go partly for the aesthetic pleasure, but also to learn about plants and design, and to loot from the plant stall, where there are often unusual plants for sale which are difficult to find in commercial centres.

On a long trip, I equip myself with maps and guidebooks and a picnic lunch, but our first expeditions would be in the neighbourhood – perhaps to the Old Rectory at Farnborough where dear Betjeman once lived. The garden was a wild place in those days, largely a scratching ground for Penelope's caponned chickens which were the size of turkeys (she doctored them herself). Today there are masses of old roses and fine herbaceous borders and an elegant swimming pool which Betj would not have cared for.

The secret of getting more out of a garden visit than an 'oo-er, isn't it lovely' experience is to go round at least twice. I go round the first time to enjoy myself and to get an overall idea of the garden, and the second time I take a lot of notes and make crude sketches, because unless you have a marvellous visual memory you forget what you have seen. How well a patch of autumn cyclamen looks under a pine tree, thriving in the carpet of needles … the yellow-flowered *Clematis tanguticus* shows up well trained through an evergreen, perhaps an elaeagnus … seeds of candytuft can be scattered successfully in paving cracks, and come up in cottagey clumps (must tell Calypso) … whatever the price, I must have more box. Colour groupings can be inspiring, too, such as black tulips with forget-me-nots, instead of boring pink ones; or white flowers with apricot, such as white roses underplanted with alstroemerias. If I carry out one idea in twenty it is a miracle, for I am short of many resources, and my garden is too thickly planted as it is, but seeing perfection gives one goals to strive for.

Let us look up the National Gardens Scheme yellow guide and fix a date. We won't go at opening time, but later, when the light will be softer. Gardens look their worst at mid-day when the sun is garish and the shadows are hard.

Anne Scott-James, *Gardening Letters to my Daughter,* 1990

When the English statesman Sir Thomas More wrote Utopia, *his vision of a perfect country, he didn't neglect the gardens. His blueprint is still relevant today – complete with neighbours warring over hedges and families closely packed together in streets furiously competing (without a word being said) to create the tidiest, busiest and generally best-kept garden.*

Utopian gardens

They set great store by their gardens. In them they have vineyards, all manner of fruit, herbs and flowers, so pleasant, so well furnished, and so finely kept, that I never saw things more fruitful nor better trimmed in any place. Their study and diligence herein cometh not only of pleasure, but also of certain strife and contention that is between street and street, concerning the trimming, husbanding and furnishing of their gardens, every man for his own part. And verily you shall not lightly find in all the city anything that is more commodious, either for the profit of the citizens or for pleasure. And therefore it may seem that the first founder of the city minded nothing so much as he did these gardens.

Sir Thomas More, *Utopia,* 1516

from The Old Vicarage, Grantchester

Just now the lilac is in bloom,
All before my little room;
And in my flower-beds, I think,
Smile the carnation and the pink;
And down the borders, well I know,
The poppy and the pansy blow ...
Oh! there the chestnuts, summer through,
Beside the river make for you
A tunnel of green gloom, and sleep
Deeply above; and green and deep
The stream mysterious glides beneath,
Green as a dream and deep as death.
– Oh damn! I know it! and I know
How the May fields all golden show,
And where the day is young and sweet,
Gild gloriously the bare feet
That run to bathe ...
    Du lieber Gott!

Here am I, sweating, sick and hot,
And there the shadowed waters fresh
Lean up to embrace the naked flesh,
Temperamentvoll German Jews
Drink beer around; – and *there* the dews
Are soft beneath a morn of gold,
Here tulips bloom as they are told;
Unkempt about those hedges blows
An English unofficial rose;
And there the unregulated sun
Slopes down to rest when day is done,
And wages a vague unpunctual star,
A slippered Hesper; and there are
Meads towards Haslingfield and Coton
Where *das Betreten*'s not *verboten*.

Rupert Brooke (1887–1915)

The politician and essayist Sir Francis Bacon was a renowned gardener, and one of his Tudor plots survives around the corner from where I live in Islington, north London. The garden is not, however, nearly as lyrical as this passage about the scent of flowers.

The breath of flowers

Because the Breath of Flowers is far Sweeter in the Air (where it comes and goes, like the Warbling of Musick) than in the Hand, therefore nothing is more fit for that Delight, than to know what be the Flowers and Plants that do best perfume the Air. Roses, Damask and Red, are fast Flowers of their Smells, so that you may walk by a whole Row of them, and find nothing of their Sweetness; yea, though it be in a morning Dew. Bays likewise yield no Smell as they grow, Rosemary little, nor Sweet-Marjoram. That, which above all others, yields the sweetest smell in the Air, is the Violet, specially the White double Violet, which comes twice a year, about the middle of April, and about Bartholomew-tide. Next to that is the Musk Rose, then the Strawberry leaves dying with a most excellent Cordial Smell. Then the Flower of the Vines, it is a little Dust, like the Dust of a Bent, which grows upon the Cluster in the first coming forth. Then Sweet-Briar, then Wall-Flowers, which are very delightful to be set under a parlour, or lower Chamber Window. Then Pinks, especially the Matted Pink, and Clove Gilly-Flower. Then the Flowers of the Lime-Tree. Then the Honey-Suckles, so they be somewhat afar off. Of Bean-Flowers I speak not, because they are Field Flowers. But those which perfume the Air most delightfully, not passed by as the rest, but being Trodden upon and Crushed, are three: that is Burnet, Wild-Time and Water-Mints. Therefore you are to set whole Alley of them, to have the pleasure when you walk or tread.

Sir Francis Bacon (1561–1626)

The points Sir Francis makes about the smell of flowers and plants are interesting. The aromatic plants which do not scent the air release their natural oils when they are crushed or brushed. Rosemary is therefore often planted by doorways so visitors release its scent as they sweep past. The plants which smell when rubbed or trodden on also release their smells in cooking, which air-scenters do not.

Epilogue Wiltshire

The painted autumn overwhelms
The summer's routed last array,
The citron patches on the elms
Bring sunshine to a sunless day.

The dahlias and chrysanthemums
Droop in the dripping garden lane,
A drowsy insect hums and drums
Across the imprisoning window-pane.

The creeper's hatchment red and brown
Falls gently on the garden bed,
The lurid snow-cloud on the down
Can scarcely hide the winter's head.

John Meade Falkner (1858–1932)

Marianne North travelled the world during the 19th century, drawing and painting people, views and flowers. More than 800 of these works of art were arranged by her – along with 246 different woods she collected on her travels – in the Marianne North Gallery at Kew Gardens in London. Here she is in Jamaica.

A painter in Jamaica

From my verandah or sitting-room I could see up and down the steep valley covered with trees and woods; higher up were meadows, and Newcastle 4,000 feet above me, my own height being under a thousand above the sea. The richest foliage closed quite up to the little terrace on which the house stood; bananas, rose-apples (with their white tassel flowers and pretty pink young shoots and leaves), the gigantic bread-fruit trumpet-trees (with great white-lined leaves), star apples (with brown and gold plush lining to their shiny leaves), the mahogany-trees (with their pretty terminal cones), mangoes, custard apples and endless others, besides a few dates and cocoa-nuts. A tangle of all sorts of gay things underneath, golden-flowered allamandas, bignonias, and ipomoeas over everything, heliotropes, lemon-verbenas, and geraniums from the long-neglected garden running wild like weeds; over all a giant cotton-tree quite 200 feet high was within sight, standing up like a ghost in its winter nakedness against the forest of evergreen trees, only coloured by quantities of orchids, wild pines and other parasites which had lodged themselves in

its soft bark and branches. There was a small valley at the back of the house which was a marvel of loveliness, bananas, daturas, and great *Caladium esculentum* bordering the stream, with the *Ipomoea bona-nox*, passion-flower, and *Tacsonia thunbergii* over all the trees, giant fern fronds as high as myself, and quantities of smaller ferns with young pink and copper-coloured leaves, as well as the gold and silver varieties. I painted all day, going out at daylight and not returning until noon.

Marianne North, *Recollections of a Happy Life,* 1894

<hr />

Artists can become inspired gardeners because they are trained to see more than just the plants or the bones of the design. Here, Robert Dash, an American painter living on Long Island, brings the winds of the Atlantic and the shimmer of blown water into his scheme.

Hero of the landscape

Although I like white on white (the 'Duchess of Edinburgh' clematis on a white fence over *Rosa* 'Blanc Double de Coubert', and I like to whiten white by throwing *Clematis paniculata* over yew and holly), the major push is for green on green. I have never cared much for all grey gardens or all blue gardens, indeed I am not certain that they are ever successful, colour being too quixotic to control in that fashion, full of lurking betrayals so that sky blue becomes sea-blue or slate blue and then not blue at all. The air over my garden from whose several points I can see the Atlantic surf is full of a most peculiar double light, rising and falling, and is itself one of the heroes of my landscape, kinder to foliage and bark than to flowers at any rate. Wild air will always do the painting. I have increased the atmosphere's multiple shimmer by putting in four small ponds above whose surfaces small mists sometimes gather. In contrast, I have made darkness with a copse of twisted, pruned Arctic willows and another of a spinny of Black pines, the former underplanted with a mix of epimedium, woodruff, Japanese wood anemones and ferns and both washed with the littlest of spring bulbs. Paths are of brick, pebbles or setts or grass and alternate curves with strict, straight geometries the better to bound, heighten and confine the predominantly relaxed, semi-wild, superabundant atmosphere I like.

Robert Dash, 'English Bones, American Flesh', *Hortus,* 1987

Somersby, Lincolnshire: After Leaving the Rectory

Unwatched, the garden bough shall sway,
The tender blossom flutter down,
Unloved, that beech will gather brown,
This maple burn itself away;

Unloved, the sun-flower, shining fair,
Ray round with flames her disk of seed,
And many a rose-carnation feed
With summer spice the humming air;

Unloved, by many a sandy bar,
The brook shall babble down the plain,
At noon or when the lesser wain
Is twisting round the polar star.

Uncared for, gird the windy grove,
And flood the haunts of hern and crake;
Or into silver arrows break
The sailing moon in creek and cove;

Till from the garden and the wild
A fresh association blow,
And year by year the landscape grow
Familiar to a stranger's child;

As year by year the labourer tills
His wonted glebe, or lops the glades;
And year by year our memory fades
From all the circle of the hills.

Alfred, Lord Tennyson (1809–92)

Helen Dillon has a celebrated town garden in Dublin and has been awarded the Royal Horticultural Society's Veitch medal for her services to gardening. She wrote a short but inspiring column in Ireland's Sunday Tribune. *I like this example because, first, it turns my prejudice against gold plants on its head and, second, it's an idea I'd never heard or seen before.*

Nothing but yellow

I must tell you about a superb piece of planting. Imagine a north-facing corner between high walls, the deeply-shaded narrow beds beneath the walls dust-dry. Gloomsville personified, or so it was, until transformed by John Bourke of Fairfield Lodge into a magical courtyard, sparkling with light and bright colour, complete with quietly trickling water into an oval basin. How did he do it?

First John painted the two concrete walls pale terracotta, the sort of shade that makes you think of Tuscany and ancient sun-baked bricks. He then attached wooden trellis to the walls to form arched niches, painted the trellis matt dark green, and built the raised oval basin of water in the middle. Apart from supporting climbers, the arches in the trelliswork prettily frame the planting. A lawn would be impossible to manage in such a position, so the remainder of the area is paved.

When you enter this little enclosed garden you're almost dazzled by light, for the planting is entirely on the theme of yellow, from bright gold to the palest primrose and chartreuse.

No other colour intrudes. The basic, evergreen structural planting consists of a pair of variegated hollies, *Ilex* x *altaclerensis* 'Golden King', standing sentinel at either side of the pool, a good aucuba, its dark green leaves broadly splashed with yellow, ivy 'Goldheart', *Choisya ternata* 'Sundance' and a large golden privet, clipped into the shape of an obelisk. The golden hop, *Humulus lupulus* 'Aureus', romps gaily along one side, reaching annually to 20 feet, entwining itself with everything else, a golden philadelphus and berberis at its feet. (An important note about many golden-leaved plants, these three in particular: in full sun their foliage is inclined to burn to a harsh yellow, but in shade the leaves are luminous lime – very nice.) The Spanish broom, *Spartium junceum*, still splendid in middle-age, sends showers of golden-yellow pea-flowers from 15 feet above. Gaunt in habit, the appearance of this shrub much depends on judicious annual pruning. An endless supply of yellow blossom is provided by *Abutilon* 'Canary Bird' and *Euryops pectinatus*, a bulging shrub with delicate ferny leaves and cheerful yellow daisies. (These last two are both tender and should only be tried outside in mild gardens.)

Annual frivolity is provided by the climbing canary creeper, with blue-green leaves and lemon flowers, plus a dashing array of golden nasturtiums. Two standard yellow roses, 'Chinatown', in white-painted square wooden tubs, mark the entrance to the conservatory opposite. Coping with deep shade at the foot of a wall and consequent dryness (walls absorb moisture like a sponge) has been dealt with by using a special hose with many little perforations, through which water seeps. The hose remains in situ throughout the year.

The large umbrella leaves of *Astilboides tabularis* were in the pink of condition, due to the presence of the hose. A known moisture-lover, this is one of the finest foliage plants you can get (it used to be known as *Rodgersia tabularis*). It was beautifully complemented by its neighbours, the golden-leaved raspberry, the golden form of *Tanacetum parthenium*, yellow Welsh poppy and various ferns.

One of the cleverest things in this small garden is the unusual use of a common plant, namely *Euonymus* 'Emerald 'n' Gold' (the name alone is tiresome enough, what with its two extra apostrophes). This euonymus often suffers the indignity of being planted on roundabouts or, worse, being used as a focal point in heather gardens. But here, clipped into squares, it was occupying no less than five square wooden tubs. I like John's idea of having foliage colour that he can move around, giving patches of sunlight wherever he wants.

Helen Dillon, *Sunday Tribune* column, 31 JULY 1994

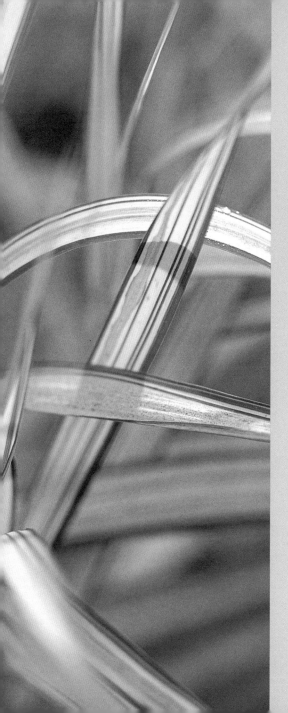

from The Prairies

These are the gardens of the Desert, these
The unshorn fields, boundless and beautiful,
For which the speech of England has no name –
The Prairies. I behold them for the first,
And my heart swells, while the dilated sight
Takes in the encircling vastness. Lo! they stretch,
In airy undulations, far away,
As if the ocean, in his gentlest swell,
Stood still, with all his rounded billow fixed,
And motionless forever. – Motionless? –
No – they are all unchained again. The clouds
Sweep over with their shadows, and, beneath,
The surface rolls and fluctuates to the eye;
Dark hollows seem to glide along and chase
The sunny ridges. Breezes of the South!
Who toss the golden and the flame-like flowers,
And pass the prairie-hawk that, poised on high,
Flaps his broad wings, yet moves not – ye have played
Among the palms of Mexico and vines
Of Texas, and have crisped the limpid brooks
That from the fountains of Sonora glide
Into the calm Pacific – have ye fanned
A nobler or a lovelier scene than this?

William Cullen Bryant (1794–1878)

Although she was gardening at the start of the 20th century, Gertrude Jekyll's ideas are still influential. In this excerpt, she describes the vegetable garden as a proper good-looking garden, where beautiful vegetables take the place of flowers. Exactly this kind of garden won a gold medal for Terence Conran at the Chelsea Flower Show about a century later.

The beauties of sea-kale

I have often thought what a beautiful bit of summer gardening one could do, mainly planted with things usually grown in the kitchen garden only, and filling up spaces with quickly-grown flowering plants. For climbers, there would be the Gourds and Marrows and Runner Beans; for splendour of port and beauty of foliage, Globe Artichokes and Sea-Kale, one of the grandest of blue-leaved plants. Horse-radish also makes handsome tufts of its vigorous deep-green leaves, and Rhubarb is one of the grandest of large-leaved plants. Or if the garden were in shape a double square, the further portion being given to vegetables, why not have a bold planting of these grand things as a division between the two, and behind them a nine-feet high foliage-screen of Jerusalem Artichoke? This Artichoke, closely allied to our perennial Sunflowers, is also a capital thing for a partition screen; a bed of it two or three feet wide is a complete protection through the summer and to the latest autumn.

Gertrude Jekyll, *Home and Garden,* 1900

The novelist George Eliot, writing in the mid 19th century,
looks back nostalgically to the simple English cottage garden.
Her longing for old roses and fruits was shared by many. By
the mid 20th century all her favourites were back in fashion.

An old-fashioned paradise

The garden was one of those old-fashioned paradises which
hardly exist any longer except as memories of our childhood: no
finical separation between flower and kitchen-garden there; no
monotony of enjoyment for one sense to the exclusion of another;
but a charming paradisiacal mingling of all that was pleasant to
the eye and good for food. The rich flower-border running along
every walk, with its endless succession of spring flowers,
anemones, auriculas, wall-flowers, sweet-williams, campanulas,
snap-dragons, and tiger-lilies, had its taller beauties such as moss
and Provence roses, varied with espalier apple-trees; the crimson
of a carnation was carried out in the lurking crimson of the
neighbouring strawberry beds; you gathered a moss-rose one
moment and a bunch of currants the next; you were in a delicious
fluctuation between the scent of jasmine and the juice of
gooseberries. Then what a high wall at one end, flanked by a
summer-house so lofty, that after ascending its long flight of steps
you could see perfectly well that there was no view worth looking
at; what alcoves and garden-seats in all directions; and along one
side, what a hedge, tall, and firm, and unbroken like a green wall!

George Eliot, *Scenes from Clerical Life,* 1858

from A Forsaken Garden

In a coign of the cliff between lowland and highland,
At the sea-down's edge between windward and lee,
Walled round with rocks as an inland island,
The ghost of a garden fronts the sea.
A girdle of brushwood and thorn encloses
The steep square slope of the blossomless bed
Where the weeds that grew green from the graves of its roses
Now lie dead.

The fields fall southward, abrupt and broken,
To the low last edge of the long lone land.
If a step should sound or a word be spoken,
Would a ghost not rise at the strange guest's hand?
Through branches and briars if a man make way,
He shall find no life but the sea-wind's, restless
Night and day.

———◇———

Not a flower to be pressed of the foot that falls not;
As the heart of a dead man the seed-plots are dry;
From the thicket of thorns whence the nightingale calls not,
Could she call, there were never a rose to reply.
Over the meadows that blossom and wither
Rings but the note of a sea-bird's song;
Only the sun and the rain come hither
All year long.

Algernon Charles Swinburne (1837–1909)

2

Designs and Schemes

In my view, no garden is complete without a clear basic design. Indeed, I go along with the English design guru David Hicks in believing that one can, at a pinch, dispense with flowers altogether, but not with the architectural bones. This is the case whether you are working with a pocket handkerchief or a large landscape. Either way, scheme first, plant later.

Edith Wharton's description of one of my favourite gardens in the world is both inspiring and exact. The Villa Gamberaia (where I once spent a couple of nights — and you can too) packs a hugely powerful impression into a tiny space. Catch it at dusk, with the lights of Florence twinkling below, for an unforgettable experience.

Every typical excellence

Before the facade of the house a grassy terrace bounded by a low wall, set alternately with stone vases and solemn-looking dogs, overhangs the vine-yards and fields, which, as in all unaltered Tuscan country places, come up close to the house. Behind the villa, and running parallel with it, is a long grass alley or bowling-green, flanked for part of its length by a lofty retaining-wall set with statues, and for the remainder by high hedges which divide it on one side from the fish-pond garden and on the other from the farm. The green is closed at one end by a grotto of colored pebbles and shells, with nymphs and shepherds in niches about a fountain. The grotto is overhung by the grove of ancient cypresses for which the Gamberaia is noted. At its opposite end the bowling-green terminates in a balustrade whence one looks down on the Arno and across the hills on the other side of the valley.

The retaining-wall which runs parallel with the back of the house sustains a terrace planted with cypress and ilex. This terraced wood above the house is very typical of Italian gardens ...

[The] patches of shade, however small, are planted irregularly, like a wild wood, with stone seats under the dense ilex boughs, and a statue placed here and there in a deep niche of foliage. Just opposite the central doorway of the house the retaining-wall is broken, and an iron gate leads to a slit of a garden, hardly more than twenty feet wide, on a level with the bowling-green. This narrow strip ends also in a grotto-like fountain with statues, and on each side balustraded flights of steps lead to the upper level on which the ilex-grove is planted. This grove, however, occupies only one portion of the terrace. On the other side of the cleft formed by the little grotto-garden, the corresponding terrace, formerly laid out as a vegetable-garden, is backed by the low facade of the lemon-house, or *stanzone*, which is an adjunct of every Italian villa. Here the lemon and orange trees, the camellias and other semi-tender shrubs are stored in winter, to be set out in May in their red earthen jars on the stone slabs which border the walks of all old Italian gardens.

The plan of the Gamberaia has been described thus in detail because it combines in an astonishingly small space, yet without the least sense of over-crowding, almost every typical excellence of the old Italian garden: free circulation of sunlight and air about the house; abundance of water; easy access to dense shade; sheltered walks with different points of view; variety of effect produced by the skillful use of different levels and, finally, breadth and simplicity of composition.

Edith Wharton, *Italian Villas and Their Gardens,* 1903

The gardens at Villa Gamberaia also inspired the designer David Hicks. 'I love the formality, the strong lines, the theatre of them, their sense of scale and above all their lack of colour.' Hicks died in 1998. I visited his last garden, The Grove, shortly after his wife, Lady Pamela, had given him a garden pavilion – designed by himself – for his 60th birthday. Just like Gamberaia, it was formal, theatrical, lacking in colour, but with added surprise and humour.

An open canvas

The Grove is essentially a farmhouse with a Regency drawing room added on. The garden I found here was haphazard and rambling, enclosed everywhere by walls and black barns which blocked the views of the country around. With the exception of some very good trees nearby and some fine stone and brick walls, I was left with an open canvas to work on. I made what is now, eighteen years later, an unusual and mature garden … My first act was to open the views from drawing and dining rooms, framing the resulting clairvoyées with lines of trees, chestnuts for the west-facing dining room, quick-growing hornbeams for the drawing room. The chestnuts I underplanted with chestnut hedges, the only ones I know of. They surround the black-painted pool which leads the eye to the Spanish chestnut avenue beyond and thence to the ride that I cut through a distant belt of trees to terminate this vista.

From the drawing room, beyond the gated clairvoyée, the focal point is a green 'tent' of clipped hornbeam on a metal frame, in the centre of two L-shaped stilt hornbeam walls with hornbeam hedges below them. Through the gates, to one side lies the cutting rose garden with two large beds of my favourite cutting roses. With their backs to the south wall are lined up twenty Chinese and Japanese tree peonies in pots.

The canal around three sides of the pavilion was formed in 1994. Over its drawbridge is the Secret Garden filled with old roses, peonies, foxgloves, lilies, hostas and salvia.

David Hicks, *My Kind of Garden*, 1999

Though the impression of the garden is architectural and lacking in bright colour, David Hicks was not averse to the occasional flower, as long as it was hidden.

A Cottage Garden

Where rustic taste at leisure trimly weaves
The rose and straggling woodbine to the eaves,
And on the crowded spot that pales enclose
The white and scarlet daisy rears in rows,
Training the trailing peas in clusters neat,
Perfuming evening with a luscious sweet –
And sunflowers planted for their gilded show,
That scale the window's lattice ere they blow,
And sweet to cottagers within the sheds,
Peep through the crystal panes their golden heads.

John Clare (1793–1864)

Garden design doesn't need to be angular and severe. You can equally well design an apparently random cottage garden – but it needs as much thought and planting as a formal one. Here is Anne Scott-James writing to her daughter on the subject.

No attempt at symmetry

By luck or flair, you have made no attempt at symmetry anywhere. Your garden consists of separate small trees or large shrubs, each in a bed with underplanting. Your Bramley apple tree has forget-me-nots and hellebores, your dry bank has broom and viburnum with alchemilla, hardy geraniums and a few bedding plants. Your bit of copse, where the trees are closer and the ground is shady, has primroses, foxgloves, and so on. This very simple idea is wonderfully workable and the curved beds have the advantage that they can be extended at any time to make room for more plants.

If I started again, I would do something like it. No straight walks, but everything gently curved, perhaps gates in the boundary hedges carrying the eye to the marvellous views of the downs beyond. My instinct is always to enclose myself, like a hibernating animal, and I have a secret fear of a theme park on the downs, with neolithic mock-ups wrecking the skyline. But even so, a more outward-looking garden on a freer plan might have been more appropriate for the site.

Anne Scott-James, *Gardening Letters to my Daughter,* 1990

David Hicks and Anne Scott-James represent the archetypal
male and female approaches to garden design. Division of
labour along traditional gender lines seems also to have applied
at Sissinghurst, in Kent, where Harold Nicolson provided the
formal design skeleton and his wife, Vita Sackville-West, added
her genius for planting. Here is Vita describing the origin of the
white garden at Sissinghurst.

The white garden

It is amusing to make one-colour gardens. They need not
necessarily be large, and they need not necessarily be enclosed,
though the enclosure of a dark hedge is … ideal. Failing this,
any secluded corner will do, or even a strip of border running
under a wall, perhaps the wall of the house. The site chosen must
depend upon the general lay-out, the size of the garden, and the
opportunities offered. And if you think that one colour would be
monotonous, you can have a two- or even three-colour, provided
the colours are happily married, which is sometimes easier of
achievement in the vegetable than the human world. You can
have, for instance, the blues and the purples, or the yellows and
the bronzes, with their attendant mauves and orange, respectively.
Personal taste alone will dictate what you choose.

For my own part, I am trying to make a grey, green and white
garden. This is an experiment which I ardently hope may be
successful, though I doubt it. One's best ideas seldom play up
in practice to one's expectations, especially in gardening, where

everything looks so well on paper and in the catalogues, but fails so lamentably in fulfilment after you have tucked your plants into the soil. Still, one hopes.

My grey, green and white garden will have the advantage of a big yew hedge behind it, a wall along one side, a strip of box edging along another side, and a path of old brick along the fourth side. It is, in fact, nothing more than a fairly large bed, which has now been divided into halves by a short path of grey flagstones terminating in a rough wooden seat. When you sit on this seat, you will be turning your backs to the yew hedge, and from there I hope you will survey a low sea of grey clumps of foliage, pierced here and there with tall white flowers. I visualize the white trumpets of dozens of Regale lilies, grown three years ago from seed, coming up through the grey of southernwood and artemisia and cotton-lavender, with grey-and-white edging plants such as Dianthus 'Mrs Sinkins' and the silver mats of *Stachys lanata*, more familiar and so much nicer under its English names of Rabbits' Ears or Saviour's Flannel. There will be white pansies, and white peonies and white irises with their grey leaves … at least, I hope there will be all these things. I don't want to boast in advance about my grey, green and white garden. It may be a terrible failure. I wanted only to suggest that such experiments are worth trying, and that you can adapt them to your own taste and your own opportunities.

All the same, I cannot help hoping that the real ghostly barn-owl will sweep silently across a pale garden, next summer, in the twilight – the pale garden that I am now planting, under the first flakes of snow.

Vita Sackville-West, *In Your Garden,* 1951

Osbert Sitwell writes with passion of the perfect design of the garden at Renishaw, his family home near Chesterfield in Derbyshire. Much of the planning was done by his father, Sir George, a superb gardener but an unpleasant man and father. The last time I saw Renishaw was in winter. It was just beginning to snow. The sky was dark but the garden, just as Osbert says, needed not a single flower to improve its beauty.

Chimneys as obelisks

The garden would be beautiful – is beautiful – with no flower blooming there. Though this lively country teems with industry, every prospect is idyllic, and chimneys in the distance become tall obelisks. Its architecture does not consist so much in stone walls and paved walks, as in green walls of yew and box. If you stand with your back to the large old house and face due south, on your left, behind and below the formal arrangment of beds and statues and fountains and yew hedges, lies the Wilderness, part of a wild garden surviving from the 18th century, with dark, mysterious cut glades, and at the end of them, far away, a golden cornfield in which in August and September you can just descry the turreted sheaves. Here in spring, when the trees are burgeoning, the ground is covered for three weeks at a time with the azure snow of bluebells, and later, in the summer, you find the tall over-weighted spires of wild Canterbury bells, no doubt descended from flowers escaped long ago from older enclosed gardens of monasteries and manors. On your right hand towers up the

Avenue, a piece of formal planting, old elms alternating with limes, surviving, it is said, from 1680. To the south, in front of you, the garden descends by level terraced lawns and green platforms, each with its piece of water, pool or fountain, to the outer green terrace, which commands a wide view of the lake, lying far below, and of a sweep of beautiful country rising up beyond it.

Osbert Sitwell, *Left Hand, Right Hand*, 1945

The great age of gardening began with the Tudors who, as in their houses, spared no expense to create the display needed to boost their royal images. Here is one view of Hampton Court.

Hampton Court

In the pleasure and artificial gardens are many columns and pyramids of marble, two fountains that spout water, one round the other like a pyramid, upon which are perched small birds that stream water out of their bills. In the grove of Diana is a very agreeable fountain, with Actaeon turning into a stag, as he was sprinkled by the goddess and her nymphs, with inscriptions. There is besides another pyramid of marble full of concealed pipes, which spurt upon all who come within their reach.

Paul Hentzner, *Travels in England During the Reign of Queen Elizabeth*, 1598

One of the pleasures of the new country houses – laid out in a
way that was not remotely defensive – was to be able to stay
there as a guest. Here is James Howell writing about his visit
to Lord Savage in Long Melford, Suffolk, in 1619.

A Suffolk park

… the park, which, for a cheerful rising ground, for groves,
and browsings for the deer, for rivulets of water, may compare
with any for its highness in the whole land: it is opposite to the
front of the great House, whence from the gallery, one may see
much of the game which they are a-hunting. Now the gardening
and costly choice flowers, for ponds, for stately large walks, green
and gravelly, for orchards and choice fruits of all sorts, there are
few the like in England: here you have your Bon Christian pear
and Bergamot in perfection, your Muscadell grapes in full plenty,
that there are some bottles of wine sent each year to the king.

James Howell, *The Familiar Letters of James Howell,* 1619

I wonder if many gardeners drop their cares, as I do, when
visiting some other plot. It is quite possible to amble around
a showpiece barely noticing the occasional weed or less than
perfect rose which, in one's own garden, would cause an attack
of garden grief. James Howell is clearly of my persuasion.

Rose Pogonias

A saturated meadow,
    Sun-shaped and jewel-small,
A circle scarcely wider
    Than the trees around were tall;
Where winds were quite excluded,
    And the air was stifling sweet
With the breath of many flowers, –
    A temple of the heat.

There we bowed us in the burning,
    As the sun's right worship is,
To pick where none could miss them
    A thousand orchises;
For though the grass was scattered,
    Yet every second spear
Seemed tipped with wings of color,
    That tinged the atmosphere.

We raised a simple prayer
    Before we left the spot,
That in the general mowing
    That place might be forgot;
Or if not all so favored,
    Obtain such grace of hours,
That none should mow the grass there
    While so confused with flowers.

Robert Frost (1874–1963)

Beth Chatto is renowned not only as a plantswoman but also as a gardener who enjoys tackling the most difficult conditions on their own terms. In various parts of her nursery in Essex, there are gardens devoted to boggy conditions, to shady woodland and, most interesting of all, to dry gravel. A few years ago she showed me around the gravel garden, bringing out a wheelbarrowful of what passes for soil in that area – it looked like clunky builder's rubble.

My gravel garden

Visitors to the garden will remember parking on the grass on the area of land which lies in front of the house and nursery entrance … In the winter of '91–'92 the site was prepared to make a new Gravel Garden. The land, about 0.75 of an acre, was ploughed and then sub-soiled to break up the hard compacted layers after years of parking cars. Next, using several long hose-pipes, I laid out the design. I had in mind the picture of a dried-up river bed, so I made the main path to wind through the centre of the irregular rectangle, forming long curving borders on either side, with room here and there for the odd island bed.

We dug a wide and deep hole to study the sub-soil. After a shallow layer of top soil, we found orange sand and gravel, hungry and dry. With our low rainfall, 20 inches a year on average, this site could only support plants adapted by nature to drought, and droughts for us in Essex are a regular feature, not an occasional disaster.

Watching the poor stone soil fall through the tines of the fork, I knew we must incorporate all the organic material we had been collecting for this project. Home-made compost, well-rotted farmyard manure, and bought-in mushroom compost were all used, spread thickly over the areas to be planted and then rotavated in, and allowed to settle. This preparation was necessary, even for drought-tolerant plants, because I do not intend to irrigate the area. Plants will have been given a good start, but then must get their roots down and survive, or not, as the case may be.

Unusual Plants, catalogue of the Beth Chatto Gardens and Nursery, 1997

Amazingly, this treatment worked – in spades. The garden is never watered and, Beth Chatto recounts, the summer of 1994 was very hot and no rain fell. When the plants looked as if they were at death's door, they were cut hard back – to rise again when the rain returned.

Of all the British monarchs, it was William III (a Dutchman, of course) who with his wife, Mary, took the most interest in gardens. Naturally, too, he liked them in the fashionable Dutch manner. The writer Daniel Defoe describes the king's visit to Sir Stephen Fox's garden at Chiswick.

The best judge

He stood, and looking round him from the head of one of the canals, 'Well,' says his majesty, 'I could dwell here five days.' Everything was so exquisitely contrived, furnished and well kept, that the king, who was allowed to be the best judge of such things then living in the world, did not so much as once say this or that thing could have been better.

With this particular judgement, all the gentlemen of England began to fall in, and in a few years fine gardens and fine houses began to grow up in every corner. The king began with the gardens at Hampton Court and Kensington, and the gentlemen followed everything with such gust that the alteration is indeed wonderful through the whole kingdom; but nowhere more than in the two counties of Middlesex and Surrey, as they border on the River Thames, the beauty and expanse of which are only to be wondered at, not described.

Daniel Defoe, *A Tour Through England and Wales,* 1689

You would think that, given the wet British climate, the French love of fountains wouldn't travel happily to Britain. But fashion is a great persuader. In the 17th century, Versailles was top of the chic garden league and much copied. Chatsworth in Derbyshire, still Britain's waterworks wonder, is described by a traveller.

No distractions, please

The gardens, very delightful, pleasant and stately, adorn'd with exquisite water works; the first we observe is Neptune with his sea-nymphs from whence, by the turning of a cock, immediately issue forth several columns of water, which seem'd to fall upon sea-weeds: Not far from this is another pond, where sea-horses continually roll; and near to this stands a tree, composed of copper, which exactly resembles a willow; by the turn of a cock each leaf distils continually drops of water, and lively represents a shower of rain; from this we passed by a grove of cypress, upon an ascent, and came to a cascade, at the top of which stand two sea-nymphs, with each a jar under the arm; the water falling thence upon a cascade whilst they seem to squeeze the vessels, produces a loud rumbling noise, like what we may imagine of the Egyptian or Indian cataracts. At the bottom of the cascade there is another pond, in which is an artificial rose; by turning of a cock the water ascends through it, and hangs suspended in the air in the figure of that flower. There is another pond, wherein is Mercury pointing at the gods and throwing up water, besides, there are several statues of gladiators, with the muscles of the body very lively displayed in their different postures.

Dr C. Leigh, *Natural History of Lancashire*, 1700

I have chosen this excerpt from Penelope Hobhouse's writings because she is describing the work of another gardener, seen through her own eyes. Thomas Church's garden in Hyde Street, San Francisco, is rightly famed for the design innovations he produced in the first half of the 20th century. Since his death in 1978, many of his ideas have become part of the mainstream.

Designs by Thomas Church

Thomas Church's garden has two distinct garden areas. In front, from a street lined with olive trees, an entrance shaded with pollarded planes … opens on to a shady yard where tree ferns grow under leafy Pittosporum. Ornamental box bushes frame an imposing double stairway at the main door. The steep upward thrust of the steps reflects the spirit of the hillside site. In the inner garden, reached by a central archway under the staircase draped with climbers, the layout and atmosphere is Mediterranean.

Outdoor living and a swimming pool were synonymous with garden existence; gardens were of simple design with plenty of functional paving and low-maintenance planting. Usually he separated the garden area from the natural landscape by clipped hedges, but native trees (in California evergreen live oaks, *Quercus agrifolia*, and madronas, *Arbutus menziesii*) shaded and protected the houses and tied them into their setting. Church's interpretation of garden design changed over the years; in the 1930s he experimented with freer forms, believing that a garden space should not have clear-cut definition; by his death in 1978 he had in many ways readopted a more traditional approach using geometric layouts centred on a house or pool. In his town gardens he placed emphasis on the architectural framework: pathways, steps, fences and trellis, using them with plants to compose a picture with as few distractions as possible.

Penelope Hobhouse, *Garden Style*, 1988

As in Italy and Spain, the pleasure of living out of doors, the need of shade, and the conservation of water are all problems which the Californian gardener must meet and answer. If shade, water and shelter can be regularly provided, the plants in these areas will respond spectacularly. This is especially the case in California, where there are virtually no seasons.

John Aubrey's gossipy accounts of the 17th century are an invaluable illustration of life as it was really lived. Here he describes the Italian garden of his relative, Sir John Danvers, in Wiltshire.

Full of irregularities

He had well travelled France and Italy, and made good observations ... he had a very fine fancy, which lay chiefly for gardens and architecture. The garden at Lavington is full of irregularities, both natural and artificial, that is to say, of elevations and depressions. Through the length of it there runs a fine clear trout stream; walled in with brick on each side, to hinder the earth from mouldering down. In this stream are placed several statues. At the west end is an admirable place for a grotto, where the great arch is. Among several others, there is a very pleasant elevation on the south side of the garden, which steals, arising almost insensibly, that is, before one is aware, and gives you a view over the spacious corn-fields there, and so to East Lavington; where, being landed on a fine level, letteth you descend again with the like easiness; each side is flanked with laurels. It is almost impossible to describe this garden, it is so full of variety and unevenness; nay it would be a difficult matter for a good artist to make a draft of it.

John Aubrey, *The Natural History of Wiltshire*, 1847

Another diarist, Samuel Pepys, is still widely read for his observations on London society in the 17th century. Here he takes a walk with Hugh May, the king's comptroller of works.

British is best

Among other things discussed ... the present fashion of gardens to make them plain that we have the best walks of gravel in the world, France having none, nor Italy; and the green of our bowling alleys is better than any they have. So our business here being air, this is the best way, only with a little mixture of statues, or pots, which may be handsome, and so filled with another pot of such or such a flower of green, as the season of the year will bear. And then for flowers, they are best seen in a little plot by themselves; besides, their borders spoil the walks of another garden: and then for fruit, the best way is to have walls built circularly one within another, to the south, on purpose for fruit, and leave the walking garden only for that use.

The Diary of Samuel Pepys, vol. 7, 1666

Pepys here is extraordinarily chauvinistic. France and Italy have perfectly good gravel walks, probably better than in Britain, where weeds spring up with such ease. And, while it is true that nothing can rival the British lawn or bowling allée, the reason lies in our wet summers, which even Pepys must have admitted could not be as pleasant as those further south.

I must have visited hundreds of gardens in my time but few have remained with me – and inspired me – as much as York Gate, an acre's worth of garden just outside Leeds into which an enormous amount had been crammed. My second visit, in 1986 – to describe it for The World of Interiors *– was as sad as it was influential. The real genius behind the design was Robin Spencer, who was far ahead of his time. He had died young five years earlier and his mother, Sybil, was bravely trying to keep the garden alive in his memory and to ensure its survival after her own death. In this she succeeded: York Gate is now run by the Gardeners' Royal Benevolent Society and opened regularly.*

But Robin insisted ...

Robin Spencer was a perfectionist. Over the years, he scoured farmyards, antique shops, auctions, demolition sites for carved stone lions, Japanese lanterns, classical pillars or troughs. Three exotic stone beasts came from the top of a safe-deposit building in Leeds and a Gothick font from the city's park director. It was Robin who suddenly discovered that the 'white' garden was out of alignment with the house. 'He decided it had to be moved by a foot,' says Mrs Spencer. 'It was a terrible job. I was told to knap all the stones with a special hammer – I had my hands wrapped against the cold. Then, when the path was in the middle, he stood back and said, "We're missing a good view – the hedge blocks it out." So we asked the next-door neighbours if we could make a gap in the hedge. That's how we created the smallest haha in the world. We planted one side white and the other silver but Robin said it looked odd so we replanted it. Then Robin got a local stonemason to create an astrolabe. And then he wanted a climax to the view from it – so we made a new window at the back of the house to look like a Gothick summer house.'

Mrs Spencer herself spends every available hour in her garden and is as concerned about the minutiae as her son. Her potting shed is immaculate and structured as a Japanese sand garden, a joy to visit and work in. Robin got a local joiner to make all the drawers for a birthday present – they were lettered in York and given brass knobs: 'I used to put things in baskets, but he insisted.'

Sometimes Mrs Spencer worried that Robin would go over the top, adding more and more architectural detail to what was, after all, a small country garden. 'To start with, we had great arguments – sometimes the committee disbanded in disorder, but we always reached agreement in the end, and eventually I left it all up to him … I have a feeling that when he died he'd really finished it.'

Leslie Geddes-Brown, *The World of Interiors,* 1987

*To my mind, one of the worst aberrations of British gardening
is the rockery. Fine if you are in the Lake District or the
Scottish Highlands – less fine in Hull or Hertford. The rockery
held sway for the first 50 years of the 20th century, especially at
the Chelsea Flower Show. But the love affair between Brit and
rockery goes back to the late 18th century, inspired by William
Beckford's writings about the Cintra mountains of Portugal.*

Nature's temple

Amidst the crevices of the mouldering walls, and particularly
in the vault of a cistern … I noticed some capillaries and
polypodiums of infinite delicacy; and on a little flat space
before the convent a numerous tribe of pinks, gentians and
other alpine plants, fanned and invigorated by the pure mountain
air. These refreshing breezes, impregnated with the perfume of
innumerable aromatic herbs and flowers, seemed to infuse new
life into my veins, and, with it, an almost irresistible impulse to
fall down and worship in this vast temple of nature, the source
and cause of existence.

William Beckford, *Italy with Sketches of Spain and Portugal,* 1787

*This holy moment seems to have led to his building of Fonthill,
'an ornamental building which should have the appearance of a
convent, be partly in ruins and yet contain some habitable
apartments' with an alpine garden in the quarry.*

Gardening is clearly a dogmatic trade, as anyone who has dealt with an aged professional will know. Literature is littered with stories of grumpy old men who refuse to allow vegetables to be picked or eaten – and who always know best, usually telling us what we've done wrong in incomprehensible jargon. Here the diplomat and essayist Sir William Temple runs bossily true to form. It is perfectly possible to create a wonderful garden without fruit, without flowers and, just maybe, without water or shade. You couldn't drop all four at once and, given a choice of two, I would pick water and shade as most important.

Four essentials

In every Garden Four Things are necessary to be provided for, Flowers, Fruit, Shade and Water, and whoever lays out a Garden without all these, must not pretend in it any Perfection. It ought to lie to the best Parts of the House, or to those of the Master's commonest Use, so as to be but like one of the Rooms out of which you step into another.

Sir William Temple, *Upon the Gardens of Epicurus,* 1685

While the French taste was fashionable throughout Europe in the 17th century, by the end of the period designers were starting to look at China, whose style was utterly different from the formal French.

Chinese scorn

Among us, the beauty of building and planting is placed chiefly in some certain proportions, symmetries or uniformities; our walks and our trees ranged so as to answer one another, and at exact distances. The Chinese scorn this way of planting and say a boy that can tell a hundred may plant walks of trees in straight lines, and over-against one another, and to what length and extent he pleases. But their greatest reach of imagination is employed in contriving figures, where the beauty shall be great, and strike the eye, but without any order or disposition of parts that shall be commonly or easily observed … But I should hardly advise any of these attempts in the figure of gardens among us; they are adventures of too hard achievement for any common hands; and, though there may be more honour if they succeed well, yet there is more dishonour if they fail, and it is twenty to one they will; whereas in regular figures, it is hard to make any great and remarkable faults.

Sir William Temple, *Upon the Gardens of Epicurus*, 1685

Sir William Chambers, who actually visited China, was much less pessimistic than Temple about reproducing a Chinese garden. As well as designing the Pagoda at Kew, he brought out A Dissertation on Oriental Gardening *(1772) and* Designs of Chinese Buildings *(1787). The* Dissertation *was, however, an attack on the landscapists, especially Capability Brown.*

The task of a century

Their gardeners are not only botanists, but also painters and philosophers, having a thorough knowledge of the human mind, and the arts by which its strongest feelings are excited … In China, gardening is a distinct profession, requiring an extensive study; to the perfect of which few arrive. The gardeners then, far from being either ignorant or illiterate, are men of high abilities, who join to good natural parts, most ornaments that study, travelling, and long experience can supply them with: it is in consideration of these accomplishments only that they are permitted to exercise their profession, for with the Chinese the taste of ornamental gardening is an object of legislative attention, it being supposed to have an influence upon the general culture, and consequently upon the beauty of the whole country. They observe, that mistakes committed in this art, are too important to be tolerated, being much exposed to view, and in a great measure irreparable; as it often requires the space of a century, to redress the blunders of an hour.

Sir William Chambers, *A Dissertation on Oriental Gardening*, 1772

When I was editing Country Life Gardens, *an annual magazine, I asked the Chelsea gold medal garden designer George Carter to plunge his rapier into garden design fashions. Fashions, or rather fads, have always had their silly side – and I was delighted when he attacked a fair few.*

The shock of the old

In gardening as in everything else it is very rare to see something completely new. What is sold to us as the latest fashion – completely new, never been seen before – very often turns out to be a slight reworking of an old favourite, just enough out of date to be temporarily forgotten. A short search usually finds that our ancestors used the same ideas, often with greater success.

If I see another drift of grasses, only looking tolerable one month out of twelve, and looking thin and without substance even at their best, I think I shall take a blade to them – or to myself. In my opinion, Gertrude Jekyll had the right idea, using grasses sparingly – particularly in blue-grey compositions where their airy insubstantiality adds to the misty effect of aerial perspective that such borders have. The word border implies a rather staid thing, but hers are bold and pictorial. At Munstead Wood she had a very modern sounding combination of Sea Kale, Lyme-grass and Santolina.

Roberto Burle Marx had already invented the large-scale ground cover drift sixty years ago and probably used it more inventively, and certainly as boldly as it is used now. In the same era (the 1930s) 'architectural foliage' (another buzz phrase) was identified or at least named, probably by M. Correlin – a Swiss nurseryman – though the characteristics of boldly sculptural foliage had been appreciated before that in Arts and Crafts borders.

Very unfortunately, Gertrude Jekyll also had a taste for the bright hot colours currently *de rigueur*. Her plan for an Orange garden in *Colour Schemes for the Flower Garden* (1908), or the red part of her summer walled garden, sound truly repellent to me, even directed by her supremely refined aesthetic sense, but they might well appeal to contemporary taste where such things are often attempted – especially at the Chelsea Flower Show – but then we do not expect to see much taste at that annual display of gardening excess. There is certainly nothing intrinsically wrong with colours in the warm range, but they can look very unfortunate in the background of British landscapes and gardens. Humphry Repton (1752–1818) developed a very useful theory that flowers in the warm colour range should only be used in the foreground of a scene – be it garden or landscape – because they visually jump forward, destroying any sense of recession if they are used in the distance.

Geometric abstraction has a much longer history in gardens than in painting. One can trace a continuous development linking strikingly minimal late 17th-century compositions of grass, tree and water to the wonderful mid-20th-century reworkings of the same theme by Luis Barragán. Today, Charles Jencks's spectacular large-scale Scottish garden brings these ideas up-to-date, linking them symbolically with new scientific research. Such ideas are equally adaptable to smaller town gardens, as my last year's Christie's Sculpture Garden at Chelsea was designed to illustrate.

Humphry Repton's designs for Claybury, Essex, from his *Red Book* of 1791 is an early example of simplification. Here he rejects the conventional 'dressed pleasure ground' of the period with its gravel walks and brightly coloured flowering shrubs in favour of a much more discreet design using native shrubs and grass paths that merge imperceptibly with the picturesque wildness of the adjoining Epping Forest. Repton, who formulated so many of the design principles of modern landscaping, combined a uniquely analytical eye for the visual effects of gardening with an awareness of what we would now call ecology.

Gertrude Jekyll's extremely refined eye for colour modulation did not stop her from using strikingly modern orange and red colour combinations, or yellow and gold – a palette favoured today by Piet Oudolf and others. Though she drew the line at the now fashionable 'raw magenta' of some geraniums she did make inventive use of fairly lurid bedding plants – scarlet geraniums, blue lobelia and yellow calceolaria – much to the disgust of many of her contemporaries, who associated them solely with outdated mid-19th-century carpet bedding.

The recent taste for grasses should be treated with caution. In large gardens such as the Old Rectory, East Ruston, they are a luxury reserved for viewing during the short time of the year when they look really good and by-passed for the rest, or mixed … with the more permanent effect of phormiums. Used in a carefully self-supporting structure of mixed grasses and herbaceous plants they can look good – but they can also look terribly messy and amorphous.

Minimalism is a much vaunted style now, and though it certainly would not have been much favoured by the Edwardians, it was fully appreciated in the late 17th century when some very cool large-scale, geometric compositions of hedge, grass and water were devised. They are, to my mind, some of the most satisfactory man-made landscapes ever devised and are more cheerful than all the half-baked naturalistic landscapes that have been subsequently cobbled up.

George Carter, *Country Life Gardens*, 2000

3
Plant Passions

Just like food and clothes, gardening has fashions. A plant becomes a star, looses its shine and falls out of favour. Then the cycle starts again. Gardeners, too, are as wildly inaccurate and contradictory about how to grow plants as they are about their qualities. One man's enthusiasm for yellow daffodils is another woman's — this one's — dislike of the horrid yellow blobs.

Since I reviewed Anna Pavord's masterwork The Tulip *(1999)*
– a book that inspired dozens of other profiles of plants –
the passage from the book that has remained with me most
vividly concerns the exotic passion for tulips demonstrated by
the Turkish Sultan Ahmed III (1673–1736). You must admit
that, as enthusiasms go, his harem parties with their candlelit
tortoises sound delightful.

Eunuchs, tortoises and tulips

Under Sultan Ahmed III, Turkey became a hotbed of floriculture.
High in the summer pastures of the Sipylus mountains above
Manisa were the Sultan's tulip fields, where bulbs were propagated
to fill the palace gardens at Ciragan, Sa'd Abad and Nesat Abad.
At tulip time, the Grand Vizier provided his father-in-law, the
Sultan, with night entertainment in the Ciragan gardens. (The
name Ciragan was derived from the word for the mirrored
lanterns that were used in their thousands to light the gardens.)
Music filled the grounds where the Sultan's five wives took air.
One of the courtyards of the Grand Seraglio was turned into an
open-air theatre; thousands of tulip flowers were mounted on
pyramids and towers, with lanterns and cages of singing birds
hung between them. Tulips filled the flower beds, each variety
marked with a label of filigree silver. At the signal from a cannon,
the doors of the harem were opened and the Sultan's mistresses
were led out into the garden by eunuchs carrying torches. Guests

had to dress in clothes that matched the tulips (and avoid setting themselves on fire by brushing against candles carried on the backs of hundreds of tortoises that ambled around the grounds).

Anna Pavord, *The Tulip*, 1999

Of all plant fads, Tulipomania must have been the most extravagant. A single tulip bulb might fetch the equivalent of a town house in Amsterdam when the craze reached its height in 17th-century Holland and, to a lesser extent, the rest of Europe. But fads always have their detractors.

Tulipomania

There is lately a Flower (shall I call it so? in courtesie I will tearme it so, though it deserve not the appellation) a Toolip which hath engrafted the love and affections of most people unto it; and what is this Toolip? a well complexion'd stink, an ill favour wrapt up in pleasant colours.

Thomas Fuller, *Antheologia*, 1655

Pinks

The pinks along my garden walks
Have all shot forth their summer stalks,
Thronging their buds 'mong tulips hot,
And blue forget-me-nots.

Their dazzling snows forth-bursting soon
Will lade the idle breath of June;
And waken thro' fragrant night
To steal the pale moonlight.

The nightingale at end of May
Lingers each year for their display;
Till when he sees their blossoms blown,
He knows that spring is flown.

June's birth, they greet, and when their bloom
Dislustres, withering on his tomb,
Then summer hath a shortening day;
And steps slow to decay.

Robert Bridges (1844–1930)

When we consider the scented garden, we dream of old-fashioned roses, lavenders and pinks. But plants can smell disgusting too. Gertrude Jekyll talks about her brother, based in Jamaica, who brought sprays of large white jasmine into the house, where it smelt exactly like a dead rat. Miss Jekyll also condemns the hideous smell of the dragon arum.

Stink of the dragon

I cannot help thinking of the horrible smell of the Dragon Arum, and yet how fitting an accompaniment it is to the plant, for if ever there was a plant that looked wicked and repellent, it is this; and yet, like Medusa, it has its own kind of fearful beauty. In this family the smell seems to accompany the appearance, and to diminish in unpleasantness as the flower increases in amiability; for in our native wild Arum the smell, though not exactly nice, is quite innocuous, and in the beautiful white Arum or Calla or our greenhouses there is as little scent as a flower can well have, especially one of such large dimensions.

Gertrude Jekyll, *Colour Schemes for the Flower Garden*, 1908

John Raven and his wife created two marvellous plantsmen's gardens, one in Cambridgeshire and one on the west coast of Scotland. I met John's widow, Faith, in the Cambridgeshire garden. (Their daughter, Sarah, has since gone on to create her own plantswoman's style.) I can vouch for what John Raven says here – we imported a whole lot of plants from Portugal with official permission and, although we waited for the due inspection, happily it never came.

Customs officer nonplussed

Since our marriage sixteen years ago, and in my own case long before that, we have had a passion for stocking our own gardens, so far as possible, with plants we have ourselves collected, occasionally in Britain but almost always abroad, in their natural stations. Of course, we never dig a plant up unless it is at least locally abundant. We have had the greatest success with bulbs, corms, seeds and, rarely, young seedlings. Few of the alpine or herbaceous plants which we have been reduced to digging up in maturity have successfully established themselves. This passion for collecting plants is, I know, shared by a large number of those gardeners in this country who have an occasional opportunity of going abroad, and my heart bleeds for the great majority of them who seem to think that it is an illicit occupation and go to any lengths, such as gum-boots or sponge bags, to smuggle their loot through customs. All you need do is to apply for a Plant

Import Licence to the Plant Health Department of the Ministry of Agriculture, Fisheries and Food … tell them the date of your departure from Britain, the countries you hope to visit, the approximate date of your return and the address to which you intend to introduce the plants, and nine times out of ten, the licence will reach you by return of post. With it will come a list of plants which it is forbidden to import, arranged both by families and countries and consisting mainly of various fir and fruit trees. Personally, I have never been under the slightest temptation to import any of them, and least of all a potato. When you brandish the precious document in front of the Customs Officer he is so nonplussed, never apparently having seen the like before, that he forgets to ask any embarrassing questions. On your return home you are under an obligation to send a full list of what you have imported to the Plant Health Department, who will by then presumably have had the permit back from the puzzled Customs Officer and be bursting with curiosity. But they are evidently tolerant of their weaker brethren, who cannot be expected to name any alien plant, and seem quite satisfied with such returns as 'twenty-two assorted bulbs, the roots of three different herbs'. They prudently safeguard their own and the national interest by reserving the right to come and inspect your trophies at their appointed destination at any time within the following three weeks. In our case this dire threat has never come to fulfilment.

John Raven, *A Botanist's Garden,* 1971

I have always loved Vita Sackville-West's romantic description of the survival of a tree which grew in the Chinese marshes when dinosaurs roamed the earth. All the more so because, ten years after Vita wrote this, my mother-in-law planted a metasequoia in her two-acre garden. It is today a sizeable tree with droopy, ferny leaves.

A metasequoia

I have just planted out a *Metasequoia glyptostroboides*. In case this name should by any chance sound unfamiliar, I should explain that it refers to a tree whose discovery was one of the romances of plant-collecting. It had been known for some time as a fossil going back to the Mesozoic era, which I understand occurred some two hundred million years ago, but as no living specimen had ever been seen, botanists assumed that it had gone out of existence at about the same time as its contemporaries the giant reptiles. The surprise of a Mr T. Wang can therefore be imagined when in the year 1946 three strange conifers were observed growing in a remote valley of north-eastern Szechuan. Their foliage corresponded to his fossil remains. Further exploration revealed the somewhat patchy presence of more, similar trees in the same area, growing for the most part beside streams in marshy places; seed was collected and, since it germinates readily, this extraordinary survivor from a fantastically distant age may now be regarded as safe for future generations in Europe and America.

It seems unlikely that many owners of small gardens will feel inspired to plant one, for its eventual height of 150 feet may prove as intimidating as its name. Nevertheless, as young specimens can already be seen growing in some public and some private gardens, I might as well describe their appearance so that you can recognise a Metasequoia when you meet one. Pale green and feathery in spring and summer, it turns bright pink in autumn, a really startling sight when the sunshine catches it. Judging by my own experience from a tiny seedling given to me, it grows very fast, about six feet in as many years, especially if planted in the damp situation it loves.

Vita Sackville-West, *In Your Garden Again,* 1953

Part of Vita Sackville-West's success as both gardener and garden writer (two books of hers come from columns she wrote for The Observer *newspaper) is that she loved the personalities of plants. Curiously, her descriptions of their human characteristics were probably inspired by the writings of Reginald Farrer, who discovered her 'rare darling'.*

The thrup'ny-bit rose

There are certain roses whose charm lies in their foliage as much as in their flowers. They are the roses whose foliage one can describe only by calling it fern-like; and by that I do not mean the ferns of woodland or damp places, but the so-called Maidenhair fern which used to be grown in company of smilax

for the decoration of dinner tables at public banquets, and perhaps, for all I know, still is.

First among these tiny-leaved roses I would put *Rosa farreri* f. *persetosa*, otherwise known as the Threepenny-bit rose. It could not be better named, for its bright pink flower is no larger than the old silver thrup'ny bit … I am told that in Burma it is known as the four-anna bit rose. The Thrup'ny-bit rose is a rare darling, a tiny treasure; not tiny as to growth, for it will go up to six or seven feet high; but tiny as to its leaves and its flock of miniature flowers in early summer. It comes from the South Kansu province of China, growing wild in the Ta-tung Alps, where it was found by Reginald Farrer in 1914. It is perfectly hardy, and renews its prettiness in autumn with small red fruits and colouring leaves.

Other small-leaved roses, all of which will make a big loose shrubby bush, are *hugonis* and *cantabrigensis*, smothered with butter-yellow flowers in May; *Rosa primula*, yellow; *Rosa rubrifolia*, whose beauty lies chiefly in the contrast between grey-green leaves and stem the colour of a Victoria plum; *Rosa willmottiae*, pale pink, usually the first of all to flower and valuable on that score alone, but with the tiresome fault of making an exaggerated amount of dead twiggy wood armed with real little savages of thorns when one goes to clear it out for its own advantage. *Rosa omiensis*, white-flowered, has ferocious blood-red thorns, half an inch long, magnificent when the rising or setting sun strikes through them, so take the hint and plant this rose where it will catch the morning or the evening light.

Vita Sackville-West, *In Your Garden Again*, 1953

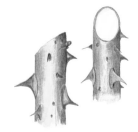

Here, I believe, is the same Reginald Farrer finding the same rose. I am not sure because at the time it had not been named. But it bears a strong resemblance to Vita's thrup'ny-bit rose.

Encounter with a yak

The next day's journey was as long as its predecessor, but seemed half, for the track wound up between narrowing mountains, with bigger heights occasionally glimpsed behind on either hand. The foothills were more and more verdant, less and less cultivated, with fresh snow on the uppermost forests of many, and, finally, at the end of the folded fells a gigantic white undulation half-way up the sky – the first highland of Tibet.

The air was alive and pregnant of marvels after the rain, the fields were filled with happy people agog with their first chance of successful cultivation in these long lean years. Busily they came and went and ploughed and sowed. I rode along in high contentment, and here at last made acquaintance with the titanic uncouthness of the yak, great patient hairy buffalo that he is, as you see him tamed to the plough. The beck becomes perceptibly more alpine as you advance, and in a bend I alighted after a most beautiful little briary of delicate tiny foliage and set all over with a dense profusion of tiny pearl-pink dog-roses. Encouraged by this, I next made a foray up into a steep oak-wood that descended on the right. The shade was delicious in the young heat of the day, but otherwise its slithering steeps of compost yielded nothing new. After this the journey steadily improves;

the sere strips of attempted culture diminish, and finally fade away altogether; and up the lateral glens and over the lesser hills more and more frequently peer forested tall points clothed thickly in solemn and enormous firs, that tower amid a fleecy haze of umber and soft violet from the deciduous trees as yet in bud, while lower down the oaks and celtis are in the first flush of their emerald loveliness.

Reginald Farrer, *On the Eaves of the World*, 1917

———————◄○►———————

Reginald Farrer has long been a hero among those who value the plant hunters. Their names live on in the plants they found – dahlia, forsythia, bougainvillea – but few remember them as people. Farrer's writing about plants made him as important to gardeners in Britain as Elizabeth David was to cooks. He was not a man for paragraphs.

An untrusted iris

Iris tectorum, in my eyes, stands far above all the other Irises, even above *lacustris* and *gracilipes*. But *tectorum* is supreme, absolutely, in his own class, which is that of the medium sized Irises. He grows abundantly on the thatched roofs of Japanese cottages, and for some reason has always been treated with quite unreasonable distrust and care in England. Import your plants from the frost-ridden Tokio Plain, as I had the luck to do, and you will find that

Iris tectorum is as incorruptibly hardy as any German Iris that ever throve in a London square. (This is the great secret of importing Japanese plants. Get them from the coldest districts, not from the South. This is how I have made such hardy perennial successes here of *Iris tectorum*, Nandina, and the Daphnes *odora* and *genkwa*.) Another thing to remember is that he will thank you richly for rich feeding; all Irises, although they look, like the lilies, so superior to earthy matters, are yet, like the Lilies, dowered with a sturdy appetite for good old rotten manure. And, with this, *Iris tectorum* will go ahead for ever on any well-drained exposed corner of the rockery. The flowers are of an unusual beauty even among Irises; the falls are broad and undulating, the standards large and spreading, so that the flower is freer and more graceful in build than the conventional Flower de luce form that you get in the German Irises. And the colour is of a wonderful soft crystal blue, dappled all over with a deeper shade; and in consistency and tone has the same waved azure that you get in a healthy bloom, when you see it, of *Vanda coerulea* in a good variety. The Iris-flower, too, has a great jagged blue and white crease along each fall, which adds to the wild elegance of its design. The white variety is as beautiful as it is rare, and the deep-blue one is only a trifle less beautiful than the clear softness of the type. And now I am twittering with excitement, for it is just possible that this year may coax a flower out of one or two seedlings that I have raised between *tectorum album* and 'Florentina'. There is a whole batch all strong and promising and some so vigorous that really I almost believe I may hope for flowers this second year of their life. However, even if they continue to grow without flowering, I shall be happy, still nursing

my anticipations of what may result from such an auspicious union. If one can only couple the free habit and unquestioned weedlike hardiness of 'Florentina' (to say nothing of its beauty) with the fairylike loveliness of *tectorum album*, both for shape and colour, a truly notable offspring should result – as, for the matter of that, should also develop from my other promising corms of the deep-blue *tectorum* with the intense violet Kochi.

Of all my little Irises, though, and with every recognition of these two last delights, *Iris gracilipes* is queen – a grassy-growing thing, forming a tuft, but never spreading along the ground, with three or four flowers carried on airy stems five inches high or so. And these flowers are, in shape, miniatures of the half-hardy fimbriate, with spreading bold falls and tiny standards. But in build and colour they are more exquisite than most things seen outside a dream, cut from the filmiest soft pale-blue silk, crumpled into half a dozen different lights and tones, with a deeper eye surrounding the pale line blotch, and following along the crest. I shall never forget my first sight of this plant. I had often seen it for sale in Japanese gardens, but had no notion where it was to be found wild. However, we went northward, I and my friends, and alighted by the way to see the famous islands of Matsushima, above Sendai, on the western coast. It was about two in the morning when we arrived, and my friends immediately carried me off to sight-see, with the result that everybody slept so firmly that the sight-seeing was not a success. Ultimately, after a lunch of rice and Worcester sauce, I laid myself down to a sleep on the matted floor of the inn, while my friends departed insatiably to ramble about and do more sight-seeing. When I awoke I found myself less somnolent and heavy, and so went out and did a little shopping in the village until my friends should return, which they did at last, showing me two withered blossoms. One was an ordinary Hemerocallis, the other was *Iris gracilipes*. Instantly all desire to eat or cavil or slumber passed away from me and with one of the explorers for my guide, I rushed off up the wooded hills to see whence he had plucked the Iris. And there at last I saw it; bursting through the thickets where Pyrolas were showing, I came out on a watery clearing from which they had cut all the hazels and undergrowth, just as they clear it in England. And there, as Primroses grow in such a place in England, was *Iris gracilipes*, abounding all down the slope in the soft rotten soil, but not to be seen anywhere else except on that one open bank. There are certain flowers that grip a hold of one in excess even in their vast intrinsic merits. Such a plant is *Lilium rubellum*, and such another was *Iris gracilipes*, whose fairylike, extraordinary daintiness of beauty as I saw it there would be almost sacrilegious and quite impossible to describe. And, in cultivation, this darling is as good as he is beautiful.

Reginald Farrer, *My Rock Garden*, 1907

I take issue with Farrer in referring to his Iris gracilipes *as a chap. There can be no more feminine a flower than an iris, which looks to me as though dressed in the brightest, best-cut couturier silk. Some plants are clearly male – guardsmen scarlet tulips, red hot pokers (no Freudian meaning intended), topiary yew – but irises, like columbines, roses and clematis, are not.*

The Rose

A rose, as far as ever saw the North,
Grew in a little garden all alone;
A sweeter flower did Nature ne'er put forth,
Nor fairer garden yet was never known;
The maidens danced about it morn and noon,
And learned bards of it their ditties made;
The nimble fairies by the pale-faced moon
Water'd the root and kiss'd her pretty shade.
But well-a-day! the gardener careless grew;
The maids and fairies both were kept away,
And in a drought the caterpillars threw
Themselves upon the bud and every spray.
God shield the stock! If heaven send no supplies,
The fairest blossom of the garden dies.

William Browne (1591–1643)

Lady Dorothy Nevill's gardens at Dangstein near Petersfield in Hampshire were renowned for their exoticism – and expensive maintenance. Lady Dorothy was a prolific correspondent and diarist, with five books – many edited by her son – of her letters and comments published after her death. In a letter to her, the plant hunter Sir Joseph Hooker describes what must be one of the first bonsai trees ever to reach Britain from Japan.

Curious dwarves

There are some curious dwarfed things among [the cases for the Queen], especially *Thuja dolabrata* with variegated leaves and a most remarkable new Damarra, also with variegated leaves, very singular. The trunk is thicker than a man's arm, and the whole tree not a foot and a half high, quite covered with its handsome foliage and innumerable little crooked branches. The trunk is everywhere grafted and every branch grafted again and again, and every one tied into its place with wire, in such manner that no trunk can be seen. Some of the pines thus dwarfed have died on the passage, and I wonder everything is not killed, for scarcely a pane in the three cases remained unbroken.

Letter from Sir Joseph Hooker,
reproduced in Lady Dorothy Nevill, *Under Five Reigns,* 1910

I make no apology for including native plants, once described as weeds, among garden flowers. We have now come to value what grows easily and naturally in our climate. Geoffrey Grigson – poet, husband of cookery writer Jane, and father of cookery writer Sophie – followed the herbalists with his own researches into the English flora. Here he describes the fairy flowers, foxglove and herb robert. The first has many dialect names.

Plants of ill omen

Bloody fingers, deadmen's bells, dragon's mouth, fairy's thimbles, lion's mouth, tiger's mouth, virgin's fingers …

Foxglove means the glove of the fox, and not the glove of anything else or anybody else. Nevertheless the Foxglove was a fairy's plant, or a goblin's plant in England (judging by its names) as well as in Wales and Ireland. The belief must have arisen from the tallness of the Foxglove, the glove-shape of the corolla, and the poison of the leaves. An Irishwoman told Lady Gregory that she knew someone who was cutting the lux more, when a fairy voice called out: 'Don't cut that if you're not paid or you'll be sorry.' An Irishman remarked to her: 'As for the lus mor, it's best not to have anything to do with that.' And another woman maintained that the los more was the only plant 'good to bring back children which are gone away' – i.e., which have been taken by the fairies. It must have been the Foxglove they had in mind. The fairy woman's los more was powerful in the matter of the children left by the fairies as well. Foxglove juice gets rid of a changeling in Scotland, in Ireland, in Wales. In Scotland, Isobel

Haldane in 1623 confessed to luring, charming and traffic with 'the ffarye-folk'. A woman consulted her about a child who was a 'sharg' or changeling. She sent her to gather 'focksterrie leaves', made tea with them, and gave it to the sharg, who died. The goblin who appears to the lovers in the thrilling Northumbrian ballad of 'The Gloamin' Buchte' looks around with snail-cap eyes, washes its hands in the dew and sings a strange, mournful song in which it mentions the foxglove … after which the goblin vanishes and the shepherd's girl hears only a plitch-platch in the stream …

In England at least [herb robert] has never been a sanctified flower. Here and abroad I suspect it was the plant of the house goblin, the German Knecht Ruprecht, our own Robin Goodfellow, the French Lutin, the Scottish Brownie, and the Black Piet of Holland; and perhaps the plant as well of the house-haunting Robin Redbreast. Robin Goodfellow was not the pleasantest of creatures, unless he was treated well and fed with cream. Knecht Ruprecht, dressing in red usually, and Black Piet, are still rather terrifying Christmas figures in Germany and Holland, coming with Santa Claus when he brings the presents, but having a stick for children who have not been good. The red-breasted Robin, too, in northern Europe, England, Wales, Ireland, Scotland, has been a dangerous bird, who brought illness, death, or bad luck when he flew indoors (a belief which is not done with by any means) … As for the names linking Herb Robert and Robin Hood, it is an old suggestion that Robin Hood grew out of elf into outlaw, and was tied in some way with the mischievious Robin Goodfellow, who haunted house and woodland.

Geoffrey Grigson, *The Englishman's Flora*, 1958

from Spring and Winter

When daisies pied and violets blue
And lady-smocks all silver-white,
And cuckoo-buds of yellow hue
Do paint the meadows with delight,
The cuckoo then, on every tree,
Mocks married men, for thus sings he,
Cuckoo!
Cuckoo, cuckoo! O word of fear,
Unpleasing to a married ear.

William Shakespeare (1564–1616)

Some of our most inspiring writers on plants are nurserymen,
especially those, like Michael Loftus, who come to growing
plants late and from love. Michael runs Woottens of Wenhaston,
a Suffolk nursery beloved by all who shop there (me included).
I've been an avid buyer of pelargoniums ever since I saw all
their exotic beauty in his immaculate poly-tunnels. Here he
explains why he loves them.

Scents of pine and lemon

Pelargoniums are a special favourite with us. We are not talking
about short-jointed bedding plants with dumpy heads of garish
flowers & predictable foliage. It is the species & old fashioned
hybrids which interest us. Their flower, their foliage & their
structure all bear no relation to the modern aberrations which
fill garden centres. Among old fashioned Pelargoniums the
diversity of the flower, leaf shape, leaf scent & plant structure
is truly amazing. Many of them will grow into large shrubs –
P. 'Purple Unique' reaches 6ft. Others have enormous leaves
– *P. tomentosum* has mature leaves 12in across. Some have leaves
which are the merest filigree – *P.* 'Filicifolium'. Some have the
daintiest of flowers – *P.* 'Fragrans' has a haze of tiny white flowers.
Others have flowers with the richest of hues – *P.* 'Lord Bute' has
intense purple-black flowers edged with red. Some are scented of
lemon, others of pine or balsam or peppermint. Pelargoniums
have many uses, apart from the traditional place on the
windowsill. The Victorians liked to bank the scented leafed

varieties on tiered staging inside glassed porches. People entering & leaving the house would brush against them, thereby releasing their scent. A pleasing salutation! The larger shrubby pelargoniums are handsome planted out in tubs during the summer or indeed in the border where their foliage provides variety of texture. It is generally held that Regal Pelargoniums do not stand being placed outside in the summer, the weather ruining the blossoms; but *P.* 'Lord Bute', one of the oldest of the regals, has been successfully planted out in summer tubs at Sissinghurst since Vita Sackville-West's day; the rich dark flowers take no damage from the rain. Curiously, 'Lord Bute' is one of the most difficult of regals to obtain.

Michael Loftus, *The Plantsman's Handbook,* 2001

I can confirm what Michael says about 'Lord Bute'. I have seen it grown in tubs in a Scottish garden, which inspired me to do the same. I planted four large pots of it – three have flourished, despite the wind and rain, but the fourth simply sheared off during a gale. I should have staked it better.

I cut out this article from The Economist *magazine because I love the idea of plants becoming living history. I am told that chives grow in the cracks of Hadrian's Wall in Northumberland – a relic of the Roman soldiers who brought the herb with them – and I know that, beside the sad crofts emptied during the Highland clearances, luxuriant rhubarb plants live on. I've often seen neglected gardens around empty houses produce swathes of flowers, from pansies to philadelphus, every year. When we found the abandoned farmhouse which is now our home in Tuscany, there were scarlet, pink and white roses blooming their heads off, although no one had given them any help for decades. The perversity of plants is such that many will refuse to seed and grow in their designated beds but migrate to the gravel all around them. Thus, the historic relics found in the stones have probably found the perfect habitat, just like their ancestors in the wild.*

Rooted in stone

According to Dr Gilbert, a botanist at Sheffield University, plant-rich walls are more than just a cheering and colourful sight. They are also a refuge for species whose natural habitats are disappearing. A score of British plants, including such rarities as yellow whitlow grass and wall bedstraw are now found mainly on walls.

Castle walls can be particularly rich. They have had plenty of time to develop interesting floras and they usually have a lot of crevices and a range of elevations from shade to full sun. Old city walls are also good rockeries. Tenby, in Wales, has 42 species per km of its medieval wall. Conway, also in Wales, weighs in with 29 per km. Meanwhile in England, York can manage only 18 per km.

Plants from arid habitats do particularly well on walls. Oxford ragwort, for instance, normally lives on scree slopes in Central Europe. It established itself on Oxford's walls in the late 18th century after escaping from the university's botanic gardens, and has subsequently spread across much of Britain. Many Mediterranean herbs, which first found their way to England with medieval monks, have also naturalised themselves on walls. The monastic physic gardens where they grew may have disappeared, but the garden walls often linger. The ruined nunnery walls at Godstow in Oxfordshire hold birthwort, once used in midwifery. Hyssop and winter savory still flower in the old physic garden at Beaulieu in Hampshire … Though some plants can prise the stones apart, a greener public is starting to demand greener walls. Plans to 'clean' the walls of Fountains Abbey, a World Heritage Site in North Yorkshire, met with fierce opposition: the common pink growing on them was part of the reason. Human history may be rooted in stone. So are many plants.

The Economist, 25 July 1992

from The Garden

What wond'rous life is this I lead!
Ripe apples drop about my head;
The luscious clusters of the vine
Upon my mouth do crush their wine;
The nectarine and curious peach
Into my hands themselves do reach;
Stumbling on melons, as I pass,
Insnar'd with flowers, I fall on grass.

Here at the fountain's sliding foot,
Or at some fruit-tree's mossy root.
Casting the body's vest aside
My soul into the boughs does glide:
There like a bird it sits, and sings,
Then whets, and combs its silver wings;
And, till prepar'd for longer flight,
Waves in its plumes the various light.

Andrew Marvell (1621–78)

The Rhodora
On being asked whence is the flower?

In May, when sea-winds pierced our solitudes,
I found the fresh Rhodora in the woods,
Spreading its leafless blooms in a damp nook,
To please the desert and the sluggish brook.
The purple petals, fallen in the pool,
Made the black water with their beauty gay;
Here might the red-bird come his plumes to cool,
And court the flower that cheapens his array.
Rhodora! if the sages ask thee why
This charm is wasted on the earth and sky,
Tell them, dear, that if eyes were made for seeing,
Then Beauty is its own excuse for being;
Why those wert there, O rival of the rose!
I never thought to ask, I never knew;
But, in my simple ignorance, suppose
The self-same Power that brought me there brought you.

Ralph Waldo Emerson (1803–82)

Christopher Lloyd has been writing a weekly column for Country Life *for nearly forty years and, despite visits to hospital, bouts of illness and tours abroad, has never missed a single issue. His books are numerous, but one of the most recent seems to combine all his acquired knowledge of garden flowers. Here he writes about cannas.*

I fell for cannas

Cannas are making a steady, if uphill, return to popularity (helped by me, I believe) after long eclipse. They were popular in Victorian bedding and thereafter survived as a tropical feature in public garden bedding schemes. Therein lay their downfall. Used unimaginatively as dot plants and quite unintegrated with their surroundings, they stick out like the proverbial sore thumb. Decried as vulgar by snooty private gardeners of the silver and grey, impeccable taste school, they languished for many years.

But their flamboyant colours combined with magnificent foliage convey a great charge of excitement which cannot be indefinitely suppressed. So they are back into the world of private gardening, their care being similar to and no more complex than the dahlia's.

I fell irremediably for cannas when I saw generous plantings in the dappled shade of trees and beside a rushing stream – in Nairobi around 1945 or '46. In that setting they didn't look self-conscious but absolutely right. Quite recently, however, I have seen them bedded in huge strips of one variety, along the central reserve of motorways in Georgia, USA, and they looked awful; the more so as a caterpillar had found them out (pests and diseases always follow where monocultures provide them with an easy living) and the foliage was in ribbons. The showier a plant is, the greater tact needs exercising in its uses.

Cannas are known as Indian Shot. They do not hail from India but from the West Indies; hence the botanical name of the commonest species, *Canna indica*. Shot, because like grape shot, the spherical seeds are hard and black … In India, a memsahib of the old regime told me that they dug up the cannas and simply made them rest on the soil surface. And to feed them while growing (for cannas are greedy as well as thirsty), 'We gave them horse; pure horse.' Meaning horse dung (in case there should be any misunderstanding).

Christopher Lloyd, *Christopher Lloyd's Garden Flowers*, 2000

Robin Lane Fox is an Oxford don who gardens and writes a weekly column in the Financial Times. *Like Christopher Lloyd, he is an original voice to which many pay attention and, like Lloyd, his expertise is lightly worn.*

A garden under the sea

I am aware how much in gardening is still open to doubt. Myself, I lost my certainties during 1977–78 in Sandwich Bay. I had planted a seaside garden for an owner with more audacity than sense. The site lay on the edge of Sandwich's silver sands, a home for Sea Kale and Tamarisk, silver-leaved Atriplex and yards of blue-flowered Hebe. In the winter after planting, the weather gave the south-east tip of England one of its hardest natural batterings. Late one winter evening, the winds fell quiet and the tide seemed to hesitate; hums and buzzes were sensed in the air, as if the whole of the Channel was on the move.

Twelve hours later, the exposed coast from Deal to Sandwich was swamped by the highest tide on record. Fences flew before the wind like startled seagulls. Ten feet of water coursed across the seaside gardens, swirled round their walls and found an entry through my patron's garden door, where it dug itself into a depth of eight feet. It sat there until the firemen ended their winter strike. So much, you might think, for the future of the south coast's seaside garden.

For ten days, maybe more, the sea water lay in the local gardens, some of them several hundred yards inland. In many,

it ruined years of ingenuity and hard labour. Plants, we all know, are said to be scorched by salt. Sea-anemones, they tell us, live under water but not, one would have thought, the Clematis, Dianthus or the Escallonia. As for the silver-leaved plants, there can never have been a winter so wet, not even in those storms which sank the Spaniards' Armada … I must report the extraordinary consequence, impressed on my disbelief by a visit some six months later. There were many odd sides to it, but the oddest was that there had never been such pinks or silver-leaved shrubs in Sandwich as those which had spent a fortnight at the bottom of the sea.

Robin Lane Fox, *Better Gardening*, 1982

*In the 18th century, auriculas were considered so special, and
their faces so pretty, that gardeners made miniature 'theatres'
for them. Each plant was displayed on a tiny shelf so that
passing visitors had a chance to admire the theatrical colours,
the mossy textures and the dramatic patterns on the petals.
It's an idea worth copying, especially in a small town garden.
Michael Loftus here describes their charm.*

Fabergé outclassed

On Easter Sunday we have a family feast. After laying the table
with an old white damask table cloth, I fill a large green enamel
basin with Auriculas to place on the table as a centre piece. No
jewels could be more stunning in the candlelight. The fashioning
of their painted faces makes Fabergé's masterpieces look like
vulgar trinkets. Auriculas were introduced into England by the
Huguenot weavers in the late sixteenth century. Gerard's *Herball*,
published in 1597, listed seven varieties. The cultivation of
Auriculas was taken up with passion by skilled artisans, and by
the eighteenth century, exhibiting was widespread. In the early
Victorian period interest seemed to fade away, but by 1870, a
sufficient revival had taken place to justify the formation of the
National Auricula Society. Today the popularity of Auriculas is
such that demand always outstrips supply.

Michael Loftus, *The Plantsman's Handbook*, 2001

from Each and All

As I spoke, beneath my feet
The ground-pink curled its pretty wreath,
Running over the club-moss burrs;
I inhaled the violet's breath;
Around me stood the oaks and firs;
Pine-cones and acorns lay on the ground;
Over me soared the eternal sky,
Full of light and of deity;
Again I saw, again I heard,
The rolling river, the morning bird;
Beauty through my senses stole;
I yielded myself to the perfect whole.

Ralph Waldo Emerson (1803–82)

Inventories have been useful in describing exactly what was growing in historic gardens. This list of the vegetable garden at Shugborough in Staffordshire was written in 1842. Pines were an earlier name for pineapples and the plantain tree was, presumably, a banana.

Small water engine, etc.

In the kitchen garden. 400 Small Pine Plants, 10 Strelitzia plants, 1 Plantain Tree, 466 Small Plants of various kinds in Pots, 6 oranges in Tubs, 77 small plants in pots, 20 Lights to Melon frames, 43 Light Frames, 6 Bee Hives and Contents, 40 Hand Glasses, 8 Watering Cans, 4 Wheel Barrows, 200 Bushels of Potatoes.

In Garden House. 6 Rush Seated Chairs, Painted Writing Desk. Greenhouse. 180 Geraniums, 24 Myrtles, 13 Arcacia Amatos, 70 Camelias, 50 Effucias, 6 Azaleas, 17 Roses, 211 various kinds of small plants, 2 Clethra Arborea, 1 Photinia Glabra, 2 Orange Trees, 2 Full length Marble Statues (Female Figures), 2 Male figures in Plaster, Small Water Engine, 63 Flower Baskets, 100 Small Flower Pots, Step Ladder.

Outside Greenhouse. 4 Painted Seats, 3 Plaster Images, Marble Bacchanalian Statue, Marble Statue of a Youth, Male and Female Statue, 1 Hand Cart Metal Roller, 1 Horse Cart Metal Roller.

In Flower Garden. 6 Painted Chairs, 2 Painted Tables, 2 Rustic Tables, 6 Hand Glasses.

Gardeners seem to make fine correspondents, constantly asking for help, giving advice and detailing new discoveries. Roger Phillips, living in a London square, established a correspondence with Leslie Land (a female Leslie, like me) who lives in Maine. What I enjoy is that the two are just as interested in food and what vegetables to grow as they are in gardens. Here Leslie writes about colourful varieties.

A vegetable palette

I'm planning a large plate of sliced tomatoes, showing off the colors of 'White Beauty,' 'Lemon Boy' (hideous name but a fine bright yellow and very nicely balanced flavor), 'Evergreen' (thick-skinned but very sweet as it turns out), and 'Nepal' (have I mentioned it? bright red slicers, not too large, good true tomato flavor and breathtaking uniformity for an open-pollinated fruit, each one baseball size and shape, big red peas in a pod).

   Also a similarly colorful assortment of potatoes, simply steamed, partially peeled and piled in a shallow basket. 'All Blue,' actually a fine deep violet, 'German Lady Fingers,' which are a pale primrose yellow inside; 'Red Gold,' the inside of which is a deep gold; 'Caribe' for its very white flesh. I may throw a few beets in here too, haven't made up my mind. The hot item in that department is 'Chioggia,' candy-striped red and white and offered by more and more chic catalogues as "an old Italian variety." They really are lovely, though not too much to write home (or to Roger) about in the taste department. And you have to serve them raw if you want to preserve the color. But the color really is spectacular. So far the best thing I know to do is to slice them very thin, like chips, and serve them with dips the same way.

There will be lots of thick green herbal sauces, natch. Basil is one place I have put the water and although the coriander has bolted in the heat, I'm planning to wow the folks by sprinkling the fish with soft green coriander seeds. They're delicious. Not sold in stores. Same like radish pods and rocket flowers.

Roger Phillips & Leslie Land, *The 3,000 Mile Garden*, 1992

I have also become enthusiastic about colourful vegetables, especially those that look wonderful in the vegetable plot and taste delicious too. I like the French leek 'Bleu de Solaise', a wonderful steely blue, and brilliant red or yellow chard, which is also stunning in a vase or a cheese sauce. My beetroot would be 'Bulls' Blood' for its bloody-coloured leaves. One of the best catalogues in which to find such treasures is Graines Baumaux, *available from Graines Baumaux, BP 100, 54062 Nancy Cedex, France (www.graines-baumaux.fr).*

I love plane trees. There is a splendid example of a plane in the French town of Bayeux, planted in 1789, at the time of the French revolution. Eleven years later, a London property developer planted a group of planes in my home square and I look out at them every morning, towering above my five-storey house. The Rev C. A. Johns, better known for his book on birds, here explains why planes are so admired – mentioning that the Persian general Xerxes stopped an entire army of 170,000 men to admire the beauty of a plane tree and hang its branches with golden ornaments.

The afternoon plane

Who would have thought it possible that a tree should have been brought from a remote region of the world for the sake of its shade only? Yet such was the case: the Plane was first carried across the Ionian Sea to shade the tomb of Diomede, who was buried in one of the small islands off the coast of Apulia. Thence it was introduced to Sicily; from Sicily it was brought to the Regium in Italy by the tyrant Dionysius and has now extended so far, that the Morini (people of Calais) are taxed for its shade …

This veneration for the Plane still lingers in the East. The great Plane of the island Stanchio (anciently Cos) in the Archipelago, is remarkable for its size and the care with which the natives have attempted to preserve it. It has stood for time immemorial in the chief town of the island; and while it is the boast of the inhabitants, it is also, and with justice, the wonder of strangers.

Earl Sandwich saw it in the year 1739, and calls it a Sycamore: 'Among the curiosities of this city is a Sycamore-tree which is, without doubt, the largest in the known world. It extends its branches which are supported by many ancient pillars of porphyry, very antique, and other precious marbles, in the exact form of a circle; from the outward verge of which to the trunk I measured forty-five large paces. Beneath the shade of this Sycamore is a very beautiful fountain, round which the Turks have erected several chiosks, or summer-houses, to which they retire in the heat of the summer and regale themselves with their afternoon coffee and pipe of tobacco.'

Rev C.A. Johns, *The Forest Trees of Britain*, 1894

—◦—

Marianne North was one of those intrepid Victorian ladies who thought nothing of climbing mountains in their crinolines. In Miss North's case, she travelled the world, drawing scenery and plants. Here she is on a second visit to the USA.

Last of the redwoods

San Francisco, where I landed on the 20th of April 1881, was in a terrible whirl and noise, and the Palace Hotel, at thirty shillings a day, was quite perplexing in its vastness … I was introduced by a Dr B. to a Bohemian wood-merchant, who told me that the finest redwood sequoias were on his place near Guerneville, many of the trees 200 to 300 feet high … The bay was most lovely as the sun rose, driving off the smoke of the big city, and I felt a new creature when I got there … Getting a train at St Quinton, and passing the pretty suburb of San Rafael, with its gardens of figs, vines and gorgeous flowers, we went through meadows blazing with patches of colour like the beds of annuals at home (only fifty times as large): nemophilas, lupins, eschscholzias, deep blue larkspurs, pink mallows, sunflowers etc. I changed cars twice, had not to wait for them. We reached the redwood forests all of a sudden, and the railway followed the Russ river through them up to Guerneville, a pretty wooden village with a big saw-mill, all among the trees, or rather the stumps of them, from which it has acquired the common name of Stumptown. The noble trees were fast disappearing. Some of the finest had been left standing, but they could not live solitary, and a little wind soon blew them down. They had a peculiar way of shooting up from the roots round the stumps, which soon became hidden by a dense mass of greenery, forming natural arbours, and many of the large old trees were found growing in circles which had begun that way; a habit peculiar to that tree.

Marianne North, *Recollections of a Happy Life*, 1894

The Poplar Field

The poplars are fell'd, farewell to the shade
And the whispering sound of the cool colonnade,
The winds play no longer, and sing in the leaves,
Nor Ouse in his bosom their image receives.

Twelve years have elaps'd since I first took a view
Of my favourite field and the bank where they grew,
And now in the grass behold they are laid,
And the tree is my seat that once lent me a shade.

The blackbird has fled to another retreat
Where the hazels afford him a screen from the heat,
And the scene where his melody charm'd me before,
Resounds with his sweet-flowing ditty no more.

My fugitive years are all hasting away,
And I must ere long lie as lowly as they,
With a turf on my breast, and a stone at my head,
Ere another such grove shall arise in its stead.

'Tis a sight to engage me, if any thing can,
To muse on the perishing pleasures of man;
Though his life be a dream, his enjoyments, I see,
Have a being less durable even than he.

William Cowper (1731–1800)

There has always been distrust between gardeners and nursery people or seedsmen. How many of us have bought, in good faith, an expensive shrub or tree only to discover that it was something quite different? In my case, an avenue of sweet chestnuts was interrupted by a whitebeam. It's an age-old battle, as this early 18th-century excerpt shows – except that, in this case, seedsman was cheating seedsman. Stephen Switzer thought he was buying wild broccoli from Naples.

Broccoli or turnip?

The greatest Difficulty that attends this Affair in getting Seeds from abroad, is the great Cheat that those People, who gather it on the Sea-side, put upon the Merchants and consequently upon us here … a great Hindrance to the using it for the Year. For though I saw the Bag just brought from the Waterside, and mark'd with an Italian Mark and Character, and saw the Bill of parcels, etc, in the Importer's own Hands, yet when it came up, it was nothing else but turneps; so little Faith is to be found amongst those Collectors of Seeds, who no doubt think it no Sin to cheat Hereticks. But in order to obviate this, I shall for the future offer no Seeds to sale which come from abroad (especially from thence) but what I try first in my own Garden.

Stephen Switzer, *The Country Gentleman's Companion,* 1720s

The Red Poppy

T.W. Gissing, a Suffolk-born chemist with an interest in botany, is brief and to the point in his poem about corn poppies. For many years the corn poppy was killed by farmers and had vanished from the landscape, but it has now made a (to me) welcome return.

—<o>—

Erect and stately, see the Poppies rise,
With crimson petals, and dark shining eyes;
They bloom above the cornfield's waving breast,
The Child's delight, and careful Farmer's pest.

T. W. Gissing, c.1850

Mrs C.W. Earle wrote her first her book, Pot-pourri from a Surrey Garden*, at the age of 61. It was an immediate bestseller, to be followed by* More Pot-pourri from a Surrey Garden, A Third Pot-pourri *and* Pot-pourri Mixed by Two. *I have chosen a note about Welsh poppies because I agree with everything she says.*

Poppy peccadilloes

July 6th – One of the prettiest weeds that we have in our modern gardens, and which alternates between being our greatest joy and our greatest torment, is the Welsh Poppy. It succeeds so well in this dry soil that it sows itself everywhere; but when it stands up, with its profusion of yellow flowers well above its bed of bright green leaves, in some fortunate situation where it can not only be spared, but encouraged and admired, it is a real pleasure. It is not a Poppy at all, but a Meconopsis. It is quite easy to distinguish between the two, once having grasped the fact that the seed-vessels of the entire Poppy tribe are flat on top, whereas the seed-vessels of the Meconopsis are pointed. There are several varieties of Meconopsis, all very desirable, and to be found, as usual well described, in *The English Flower Garden* (NB – William Robinson's seminal book).

Mrs C.W. Earle, *Pot-pourri from a Surrey Garden,* 1897

All the most distinguished gardeners insist that they never stop learning about plants – and that they never, ever feel expert. Here is Canon Ellacombe, who lived for 68 years at the vicarage at Bitton, near Bristol, where he was born and gardened, proving the point.

Shooting stars

The more I study flowers, the more I feel how little I know about them, and especially how very little is known of a plant by its flowers only. The young shoots of a plant when it first breaks the ground are often of a wonderful beauty, and are in many cases so utterly unlike the same leaves when come to maturity, that to describe a plant by its mature leaves only is to tell less than half its story. And this is only one of the wonders of young plant life. People sow seeds and watch for the coming of the plant, but few note that every separate plant has its particular method of coming out of darkness into light, and we may be quite certain that the particular method is the only one suitable to it. But the greatest mystery of this bursting forth of the plants is that it is done when the growth is at its tenderest age; when the shoot is tender and brittle it has power to push through everything that binds it down.

Canon H.N. Ellacombe (1822–1916)

4

The Gardeners

*If gardeners have one thing in common, it is their strangeness.
I suppose you can't devote your life to plants without being
driven mad and unworldly. Who but a plant hunter could die
for a primula? Who but a garden designer could condemn all
flowers? Many gardeners are bombastic, grumpy know-it-alls.
Even the sweetest old lady will kill slugs with sadistic delight.*

*Osbert Sitwell's beautiful prose doesn't conceal the dislike
he felt for his father, Sir George – perhaps because the wildly
extravagant father was constantly complaining about his son's
spendthrift ways. Unwillingly, however, Osbert admired the
gardens Sir George created at Renishaw, in Derbyshire, which
today are lovelier than ever.*

Sir George Sitwell

He walks up and down, surveying his work, which will never be
finished, his head full of new projects of sun and shade, but never
of flowers, measuring the various views with a stick to his eye or a
pair of binoculars. Sometimes he is planning a boat of stone upon
the lake, or a dragon in lead, writhing for a quarter of a mile
through its level waters, or a colonnaded pavilion upon another
island, or a Roman aqueduct in counterfeit to frame the prospect
with its elongated arches, or a cascade to fall down a stone
channel for a hundred and fifty feet, from the water to the garden
below: and, for projects such as these, though most of them never
materialised, he would cause wooden towers, built up of planks
and joists and beams – like an early machine for siege warfare or
a drawing by Piranesi – to be erected here and there at the right
point of vantage. In the summer he would spend many hours
aloft on these platforms, with a large grey hat or grey umbrella to
shield his light-coloured skin and eyes from the sun, and with a
telescope to his eye, enjoying the air and also, perhaps, the feeling
of command which such an altitude above the ground affords.

Osbert Sitwell, *Left Hand, Right Hand*, 1945

Napoleon is still not liked on Elba. For a start, he didn't enjoy its charms enough to stay, escaping after only ten months' exile on the island; and, second, he spent those months overturning centuries-old customs. His passion for detail and change – and cost-effectiveness – can be seen in this extract from a letter to Grand Marshall Bertrand. The gardens on Elba to which he refers are now charming, by the way.

The power of command

I have had your report on the supplementary expenses for September … Gardens: The man who is employing three men all month on a garden the size of my hand plus eleven grenadiers to load a few cartfuls of earth should be reprimanded. Nor do I approve of the proposed cost for turf during October; I consider grass seed to be better. Tell the gardener to negotiate with the grenadiers so that they are paid for loading the earth by the cubic metre and have just enough carts so their work is constant. This should not cost more than 80 francs. The officer commanding the engineers should also negotiate with the grenadiers over excavating the gardens. I estimate this should cost 400 francs. A total of 480 francs should therefore be allowed under the expenses for October.

Napoleon Bonaparte, 15 OCTOBER 1814

We have all at some time met fearsome gardeners – and Helen Dillon's description of Miss Otway-Ruthven brings to mind a Welsh woman gardener (and colonel) I was told about who barked with the best of them and regularly set her tweed jackets alight with cigarette stubs. On one occasion, she injured her eye while gardening and insisted on being taken to the village doctor in her capacious wheelbarrow, steered by the head gardener.

Miss Otway-Ruthven – victrix

Only the other day, I was about to dig up a sempervivum, when I thought I heard 'Don't touch that', the words coming from just over my left shoulder, accompanied by a whiff of tobacco. The plant had been given to me in the 1970s by Miss Otway-Ruthven, the late professor of medieval history at Trinity College, Dublin, without doubt one of the most formidable women of Irish horticulture. I could almost see here standing there, resplendent in one of her tweed suits of the exceptionally itchy Harris variety – I don't think she ever wore anything else. A vivid streak of orange in her otherwise white hair bore witness to the fact that she was a dedicated smoker – this much we had in common. I remember going to have tea with her – a proper, old-fashioned tea, you understand, with scones and cake and thin bread and butter, brought in by the maid. We sat by the fire, me on the edge of the chair. Conversation was limited.

Miss Otway-Ruthven was not a believer in small talk, and I was desperate for something intelligent to say about medieval history. The agonies of tea over, we withdrew outside.

In a garage at the end of the garden, seeds from obscure horticultural societies of the world over were sprouting on the dimly lit, cobwebby windowsill of a Rathgar garage, in yoghurt pots, margarine cartons and other assorted containers. Miss Otway-Ruthven, albeit the most formidable woman I've ever met, complete with intimidating bulk and growling voice, had a passion for rare seeds. I've now changed my mind about digging up the sempervivum, so vividly does it recall that afternoon.

The second ghost I never actually met in the flesh. Miss Ellen Willmott is well-known for *Eryngium* x *giganteum*, known as Miss Willmott's ghost. But you may not know *Potentilla nepalensis* 'Miss Willmott', a modest plant with cherry-red flower … Such innocence belies its name, for Miss Willmott was, by all accounts, thrustingly ambitious and rather unpleasant. She was known to inspect the trugs of her less experienced gardeners, picking out anything she didn't consider a weed. She is also accredited with the damning remark (made after a visit to a garden she considered poor): 'It is most fortunate that the owner is completely satisfied with it.' Botanists now say she had no right to name the potentilla after herself, as it's only a variant of the species. Just another attempt at self-promotion.

The shade of Miss Jekyll is ever present. I hear the scrape of her boot behind me whenever I'm planting. Whistled on the wind I hear 'Quite the wrong colour,' or 'It won't do here,' followed by the tap of a disapproving stick. But some of the exalted lady's recommendations have proved more like those of her alter ego, Miss Hyde. For example, she was fond of the blue lyme grass, *Leymus arenarius*, a dangerous coloniser, with the intemperate instincts of scutch grass. The spiky leaves are indeed a beautiful light blue (and it makes an exellent stabliser for sand dunes, for which nature intended it), but I would only dare to grow it in a bottomless dustbin, sunk to the rim in the soil.

Helen Dillon, *Sunday Tribune* column, DECEMBER 1994

Helen Dillon is probably right about Miss Willmott, who was said to be the single reason why the Royal Horticultural Society (RHS) resisted women committee members for so long. I distinctly remember noticing, while scouring the RHS minutes before writing my book about the Chelsea Flower Show, the number of times she puts herself forward only to be beaten back by the all-male committee. I'm not certain, however, that Gertrude Jekyll was a dragon. Edwin Lutyens, her protégé, seems to have loved her deeply.

David Hicks was a passionate perfectionist who designed everything around him – and around others, too – till no infelicity (as I'm sure he would have called it) could be found. When I interviewed him about the pavilion he designed for himself at The Grove in Oxfordshire, he was at once funny, informative, dogmatic and terrifying. Here is a list of his garden hates, to which he added a longer (but not much longer) list of his loves. Somehow I found the hates far more convincing.

Cultivating hatred

I am afraid that, as I have grown older, my original hates have multiplied: turquoise swimming pools, rotating summer houses, sitting room-type conservatories, cement rabbits, irregularly shaped plastic ponds, paths and pools shaped like intestines, plant labels everywhere, hoses left out, crazy paving, wood stained a revolting orange, mini lanterns in wrought iron, orange or green floodlighting, asphalt paths, inexpensive wrought iron gates and 'decorative' wells. White plastic garden chairs, grey gravel, bird baths, concrete balustrading, hanging baskets, and small fountains are all abominable.

In the plant world I have a loathing for flowerbeds, rockeries, aster, aubretia, almost all marigolds, tapestry hedges, arboretums, mixed avenues, orange lilies, forsythia, valerian, scarlet geraniums and salvias, aubergine-coloured shrubs, fuchsia, lupins, Michaelmas daisy, red hot poker, lavatera, impatiens, snapdragons, begonia, Leylandii hedges, pampas grass, dahlias, gladioli, and the year-round commercial chrysanthemums.

I could happily do away with any variegated or bicoloured plants, shrubs and trees; it's their indecisiveness that I detest – they have been encouraged not to make up their minds. Really good herbaceous planting can be superb, as at Buckingham Palace or New College Oxford, but on any less high plane, herbaceous borders are a nightmare and extremely labour intensive.

David Hicks, *My Kind of Garden,* 1999

One can only say, 'Phew.' I disagree with lots of this – I like lupins and scarlet geraniums and red hot pokers. And I don't think the borders at Buckingham Palace are nearly as good as they could be.

London Kewriosity

*Although women have been gardeners since Eve ate
the apple, they were as rare as women soldiers in the
professional field of the great nurseries and estates. All that
changed in the early 20th century. By 1908 Britain had
seven colleges for training women gardeners, and women
head gardeners finally won approval when their male
counterparts were sent to the front during the First World
War. At Kew Gardens, even before the turn of the century,
women gardeners dressed in bloomers, which created much
excitement among male tourists. Here is a poem about the
sensation, published in 1900 in* Fun *magazine.*

They gardened in bloomers, the newspapers said;
So to Kew without warning all Londoners sped;
From the roofs of the buses they had a fine view
Of the ladies in bloomers who gardened at Kew.
The orchids were slighted, the lilies were scorned,
The dahlias were flouted, till botanists mourned,
But the Londoners shouted, 'What ho, there! Go to;
Who wants to see blooms now you've bloomers at Kew.'

Artists make good gardeners. Monet is an obvious example, but John Piper and John Nash were both gardeners, and Gertrude Jekyll was a painter before she became a famous plantswoman. Robert Dash is an American painter who has gardened on the same plot in Long Island for more than 20 years.

That's torn it

Madoo, which in an old Scots dialect means My Dove, is the name of my garden of 1.91 acres and I have been at it now for twenty years. I have gone about it as I would a painting, searching for form rather than prefiguring it, putting it through a process more intuitive than intellectual. The blunders are there to learn from; the successes, more often than not, are the result of bold throws. I started from the house and went out towards the edges, often revising solid achievements until they seemed made of finer matter, like marks and erasures of work on paper which sometimes may be torn and fitted again in collage. Black pine, privet and Russian olive form the windbreak, pruned to show their fine trunks and branches, husbanded at their base by a carefully controlled invasion of Golden rod, chicory, Joe Pye weed and milkweed among which I have planted a variety of thalictrum, rhododendron and kalmia. *Lonicera flava* go up white birch. Pebbled areas, through which soar *Lilium canadense*, have brick setts for easier walking and small trickles of santolina, rue and grasses. I am particularly fond of *Molinia* 'Windspiel'.

Robert Dash, 'English Bones, American Flesh', *Hortus,* 1987

*The National Portrait Gallery in London recently held an
exhibition on* Five Centuries of Women and Gardens.
*To me, it was a revelation and ever since I've been unable to
ignore the largely forgotten female input into British gardens.
But one passage in the catalogue truly shocked me, especially
since I had seen similar masculine dominance at first hand.
Our first garden was around a small cottage in a Yorkshire
village. The cottage opposite was bought by a lawyer and his
wife. She was passionate to create a garden but he decreed the
whole should be turfed – and refused to allow her any money
to buy plants. The same brutality was practised 250 years ago,
when feminine flower gardens were demolished to make way
for masculine landscaped parks in the 18th century.*

A woman's plot

Women were intended to learn only those accomplishments
useful in married life: dancing, sewing and singing, as well
as how to run a household. Too much masculine knowledge
was unfeminine and might prevent a girl from making a good
marriage … Traditionally, the female space was the flower garden.
Increasingly, flower and kitchen gardens, along with the domestic
parts of the house, were banished from the front of the building.
To be a gentleman was to possess an estate, to look out on far-
distant prospects, both sure and certain signs of economic and

social success. To be a gentlewoman was to cut the roses in the flower garden, safely tucked away behind the house, and to be part of, rather than possessor of, the landscape.

Sue Bennett, *Five Centuries of Women and Gardens*,
National Portrait Gallery catalogue, 2000

---◦---

Women in the 19th century had virtually no rights – every penny a woman owned became the property of her husband on marriage. (When the feminist Millicent Fawcett had her purse stolen, the charge sheet declared that the few shillings in it were her husband's.) This did not mean that women were powerless, however. Lady Dorothy Nevill (1826–1913) seems to have got her own back neatly.

Lady Dorothy's revenge

In 1847, at the age of twenty-one, the witty, vivacious and beautiful Dorothy Walpole was compromised in a Hampshire summer-house by George Smythe, an experienced rake and Tory politician. He suffered no long-term effects from the incident but Lady Dorothy's reputation was ruined … Dorothy was hastily married off to her cousin, Reginald Nevill, who was twenty years her senior. In 1850, Reginald bought Dangstein, a neo-Grecian house near Petersfield in Hampshire. He started improving the woodlands and the park, while Dorothy took up horticulture in the twenty-three acres of gardens, with thirty-four gardeners to help her.

In total, Dorothy built thirteen greenhouses, together with peach and orchid houses, and melon and cucumber pits. She had kitchen gardens, with apples, pears, plums and vines fanned over the walls and a 'pinetum' with wellingtonias, a monkey-puzzle and all kinds of fir trees. There was a menagerie as well, with lovebirds in aviaries and a flock of doves with whistles tied to their tails. Dorothy also bred silk worms, at first in the house, where they crawled up the gentlemen's trouser legs, and then at a silk farm in the garden.

The plant collection at Dangstein became famous and new specimens were sent from all over the world. Dorothy had a particular interest in studying the habits of insectivorous plants and was soon corresponding with noted scientists such as Sir William Hooker at Kew and also with Charles Darwin at Downe in Kent, to whom she sent orchids, earthworms, snails and bladders.

In 1878, when Reginald died, he was no longer a wealthy man. Dorothy and economic recession had eroded his fortune.

Sue Bennett, *Five Centuries of Women and Gardens,*
National Portrait Gallery catalogue, 2000

*Some 19th-century gardens were famous devourers of money.
Here Miriam Rothschild, the inspiration for the 20th-century
interest in wildflower meadows (she encouraged the Prince of
Wales to create one), explains her family's passion for gardens.*

How to spend a million

Their gardens were probably the Rothschilds' most expensive
hobby, despite the fact that in the last century labour was
available at relatively low wages. Nathan left his widow an
annuity of £20,000, which today would have the purchasing
power of £880,000. Hannah could, therefore, afford to create
a beautiful garden in which she entertained many distinguished
guests and romped with her grandchildren.

Alice (who inherited Waddesdon from her brother in 1898)
spent approximately £7,500 on the gardens and £6,200 on the
grounds and plantations annually. These figures did not include
expenditure on painting and general repairs to the glass houses,
nor on the tools and implements. The biggest extravagance, apart
from the gardens, was on the farm and dairy, which cost £4,168.
In 1907, the purchasing power of one pound was equal to
£44 today, and thus Alice was spending well over half a million
pounds each year [on Waddesdon alone] … in today's currency,
Alice – who had no family – spent over a million pounds
annually on her gardens. These were her children …

[Marcel Gaucher, the head gardener] pointed out that Alice was a spinster with a taste for authority, gifted with a high IQ, an astonishing memory and a terribly autocratic personality. She had fallen in love with the Mediterranean flora in 1887 and thereafter spent six months of the year (October to March) on the Riviera. He considered her a born landscape gardener, a passionate botanist with an exceptional eye for the design of garden arrangement, and she herself ferreted out the finest specimen trees and plants, which she discovered in various nurseries and horticultural centres, and for which she paid top prices.

Marcel Gaucher mentioned the apocryphal tale that during Queen Victoria's visit to the Villa, named in her honour, Alice peremptorily ordered her off a corner of the garden for fear of her trampling upon some rare and precious plant – after which the Queen nicknamed her 'the All Powerful'.

Miriam Rothschild, Kate Garton, Lionel de Rothschild,
The Rothschild Gardens, 1996

I was asked to interview Miriam Rothschild for The Daily Telegraph *and found her at once alarming and exciting to talk to. As I left, I asked if I could look around her famous wild garden at Ashton Wold, which was, after all, the point of visiting her at home. 'Certainly not!' she barked. But she finally relented and let me walk around. Wild it certainly was.*

Nigel Colborn was another writer to interview Miriam Rothschild – who, I imagine, gets a trifle bored with so many of us knocking on her door.

A perfect antidote

In spite of her passion for nature, Miriam Rothschild is the perfect antidote to the muesli, beard and sandal brigade. Her philosophy is earthy and pragmatic and her wit sharp as a needle. She is still actively engaged on a staggering number of scientific research projects. Over lunch, for example, we discussed the egg-laying habits of cabbage white butterflies and their ability to detect cardenolides on wallflower foliage through sensors on their forelegs. But unlike so many eminent scientists, she has a mind so broad and versatile that in conversation every topic is snatched up, analysed and tossed about in a way which is simultaneously stimulating, enlightening and entertaining. After lunch at the pub and a short car ride back to the house, during which I sat in the passenger seat of her car under the heap of ferocious dogs, it was time to leave her. I have seldom felt such sharp withdrawal symptoms after so brief an acquaintance.

Nigel Colborn, *Hortus,* 1980

One cannot read about the plant hunters, botanists and artists who travelled the world in the 18th and 19th centuries without enormous admiration for their dedication, bravado and sheer courage. Among them was Marianne North, a gently bred, unmarried, middle-aged lady who set off on her travels in 1871 and spent thirteen years criss-crossing the world and painting what she saw. This is her encounter with Borneo.

Dining with the Dyaks

I began my return journey badly, for my pony displaced a plank in one of those horrid bridges, took fright, ran away and tumbled me off, the Rani's new saddle having no off pommell, and I lost my spectacles in a bank of fern. My friends were too frightened to let me risk the other slippery bridges, and got a canoe with a mat and pillow, and two Dyaks to paddle and push; so I gained once more the pleasure of shooting the rapids, lying on my back and looking at the tangled branches overhead, with their wonderful parasites; sometimes shooting swiftly down through deep green water and white foam, while the men clutched at the rocks and tree-stumps – sometimes being almost carried by them over a few feet of water ... I was left to stay three days with the young manager of the antimony mines at Busen, where I spent my mornings up the river in a canoe, sketching strange trees and a bamboo bridge. We saw some grand specimens of the Tappan trees, with their smooth white stems, on which bees delight to build their nests. No beasts or reptiles can climb these trees, only the Dyaks beat the bees by building clever ladders with bits of bamboo … The steam launch came up for me and carried me far too fast down the beautiful broad river again. At one point we saw a water-snake full twelve feet long, with its head held nearly a foot out of the water, swimming across most gracefully. It was all red and green, with a sharp ridge down its back.

Marianne North, Recollections of a Happy Life, 1894

When I read this, I compare her bravery (she even calls her memoirs 'a happy life') with the way we live now. Chestnut trees are felled in case conkers fall on our heads and secateurs come with a warning that they might cut. I do believe a prickle of risk, a suggestion of danger, greatly adds to our fun. Trekking with headhunters, however, is at the far edge of risk.

Many women see cooking and gardening in a similar light.
Often a good rotted compost is compared to a fruit cake. Here
Helena Rutherford Ely, a founder member of the Garden Club
of America, compares watering with making soup.

It's like soup

The watering of a garden requires nearly as much judgment as
the seasoning of a soup. Keep the soil well stirred and loose
on the surface, going through the garden, where possible, with a
rake; and if there is no room for a rake, stir gently with a trowel
every five days or once a week. In this way moisture will be
retained in the soil, since the loose earth acts as a mulch.

When watering, be generous. Soak the plants to the roots;
wet all the earth around them, and do it late in the afternoon,
when the sun is low. How often have I been obliged to chide
the men for watering too early in the afternoon, and not doing
it thoroughly, for, upon stirring the ground, I would find that
the water had penetrated but a couple of inches. During long
periods of dry weather, the garden, without water, will simply
wither and burn.

Helena Rutherford Ely, *A Woman's Hardy Garden*, 1903

*When I wrote a history of the Chelsea Flower Show, I was
as much entertained by the people involved as by the plants
(perhaps this shows that I am not a truly dedicated gardener
to the exclusion of all else). One of the most entertaining was
Lady Christabel Aberconway, who had to take an extremely
reluctant King George V around the show. While the royals have
always supported the show and visited it on the Monday
afternoon, some have been keener than others.*

A monkey for the king

In *A Wiser Woman?* Lady Christabel Aberconway (Christabel
McLaren) well recalled that frightening day when King George
was accosted by several newspaper photographers. He growled,
'This is intolerable, intolerable. They've taken quite enough
photographs of me today; these journalists, these journalists –
I'm going back to the Palace.' Lady Christabel, obviously no soft
touch, boldly reminded him that he had, after all, ennobled three
press barons, Beaverbrook, Northcliffe and Rothermere. 'It was
touch and go,' she wrote in her memoirs. 'Going through the
big tent he pointed to some mauve and orange flowers packed
close together. "Horrid colours. Pink and blue, pink and blue,
those are the colours that should always go together." I then
scored another mark. "Well, sir," I said, "I took my young
daughter to the zoo the other day and tried to prevent her seeing
certain portions of a monkey's anatomy, but she observed the

creature and asked in a carrying voice, 'Are those pink and blue patches meant to be the monkey's bottom?'" This delighted King George and, after that, every year he came to Chelsea, he told me how much he had enjoyed that afternoon.'

Leslie Geddes-Brown, *Chelsea: The Greatest Flower Show on Earth*, 2000

The Hanoverian kings were clearly blind to artistic things: King George V's ancestor George III apparently accosted Edward Gibbon when he was writing The Decline and Fall of the Roman Empire *with the immortal words 'Scribble, scribble, scribble, eh, Mr Gibbon,' while I recently heard that George VI, having seen the characteristic thunderclouds over all John Piper's drawings of Windsor commissioned by his rather cleverer wife, Queen Elizabeth, said to the artist, 'Shocking bad luck with the weather, eh, Mr Piper?'*

I love my greenhouse for the same reasons William Cowper apparently loved his – plus the fact that it is a refuge from real weather and real work. I came late in my gardening life to seed propagation, but now I always visit the greenhouse before any other part of the garden. It is an enormous thrill to see the first green shoots appear in those seed trays, to be followed so quickly by others that the entire surface of the compost is raised in the air.

An agreeable hum

I sit with all the windows and the door wide open, and am regaled with the scent of every flower, in a garden as full of flowers as I have known how to make it. We keep no bees, but if I lived in a hive, I should hardly hear more of their music. All the bees in the neighbourhood resort to a bed of mignonette opposite to the window, and pay me for the honey they get out of it by a hum, which, though rather monotonous, is as agreeable to my ear as the whistling of the linnets. All the sounds that Nature utters are delightful, at least in this country.

William Cowper (1731–1800)

Afton Water

Flow gently, sweet Afton, among thy green braes,
Flow gently, I'll sing thee a song to thy praise;
My Mary's asleep by thy murmuring stream,
Flow gently, sweet Afton, disturb not her dream.

Thou stock dove whose echo resounds thro' the glen,
Ye wild whistling blackbirds in yon thorny den,
Thou green crested lapwing the screaming forbear,
I charge you disturb not my slumbering Fair.

How lofty, sweet Afton, thy neighbouring hills,
Far marked with the courses of clear, winding rills;
There daily I wander as noon rises high,
My flocks and my Mary's sweet cot in my eye.

How pleasant thy banks and green valleys below,
Where wild in the woodlands the primroses blow;
There oft as mild ev'ning weeps over the lea,
The sweet scented birk shades my Mary and me.

Thy chrystal stream, Afton, how lovely it glides,
And winds by the cot where my Mary resides;
How wanton they water her snowy feet lave,
As gathering sweet flowerets she stems thy clear wave.

Flow gently, sweet Afton, among thy green braes,
Flow gently, sweet River, the theme of my lays;
My Mary's asleep by thy murmuring stream,
Flow gently, sweet Afton, disturb not her dream.

Robert Burns (1759–96)

What to pick from such a prolific and inspiring garden writer as Christopher Lloyd and one who relishes flouting the conventions? I've chosen – perhaps flouting a convention myself here – a couple of paragraphs in praise of hand weeding from the master of the unexpected. It comes from one of his most influential early books, which was a major inspiration to me in my very first garden.

Hand weeding

Weeding on your hands and knees means that your eyes are close to the ground – the scene of operations. They should always travel just ahead of the trowel point so that the unusual can be observed before it is destroyed. I never like to weed out anything that I can't identify. Not all seedlings are weeds. You may feel that life is too short to leave a seedling in till it's large enough to identify. My own feeling is that life's too interesting not to leave it there until you can identify it. Taking this view, you will very soon learn to recognise weed seedlings when they are no larger than a pair of seed leaves. The not so easily identified ones will then most probably turn out to be the progeny of some of your border plants or shrubs, and it may suit you to save and grow them on.

For instance, the elegant and feathery mauve *Thalictrum dipterocarpum*, revelling in a nice wet soil like ours, is a herbaceous plant that never needs disturbing and does not readily lend itself to division anyway. But in early summer you will nearly always find its seedlings in the neighbourhood of old plants. They can be pricked out into a seed box and, later on, lined out, and they may even, given individual treatment, carry a few blooms in their first autumn. *Mertenensis virginica* is another plant with the welcome habit of self-sowing. The seed leaves are shaped like spades in playing cards, and are glaucous. Here again, if the seedlings are pricked out, they will develop very quickly and continue to grow long after the parent plants have died off for the season.

Christopher Lloyd, *The Well-Tempered Garden,* 1970

I find it surprising that Christopher Lloyd seems to use a trowel for weeding. To me, a small, two-pronged fork – apparently designed by Gertrude Jekyll – is much more efficient for the purpose. Other than that, I agree that seedlings so discovered add to life's enjoyment and, being half Scots, I also like the idea of finding something for nothing.

How nice it would be to enjoy weeding – the bugbear of most gardeners. I can see that it could be satisfying in the same way that ironing a pile of laundry is satisfying. Chaos is replaced by order. But, as far as I am concerned, that is only in theory. To Anna Lea Merritt, an American artist who moved to Hampshire on her marriage, it was a genuine pleasure.

Weeding as therapy

A really long day of weeding is a restful experience, and quite changes the current of thought. For some people it is more efficient than a rest cure. It is pleasantest to take a nine-hour day of such work when the earth is wet, or even in rain, because weeds come up more easily, root and branch, from wet earth. I never want an hour at noon for dinner, like the hired man, but would prefer to lunch like horses from a nosebag. It would save time, and especially the necessity of cleaning oneself. After such a day my fingers are bleeding, knees tottering, back bent, dress muddy and soaking and shoes an offence to my tidy maid; but I have attained the most profound inward peace, and the blessed belief of having uprooted all my enemies.

Anna Lea Merritt (1844–1930)

Military men make military gardens. Lord Carrington,
the former British Foreign Secretary, who has a fine garden
in Buckinghamshire, told me that he loved disciplining plants
and getting his vegetables to stand in a row. Here W. Carew
Hazlitt, grandson of the English essayist William Hazlitt,
describes one of Cromwell's generals.

Tulip Lambert

General Lambert, who was lord of the manor of Wimbledon
in 1656, was very fond of his garden at that place, and grew,
it is said, the finest tulips and gilliflowers procurable. It is to his
passion for this pursuit that he owed his place on a pack of
satirical cards published during the Commonwealth, where the
Eight of Hearts bears a small full-length of him, holding a tulip
in his right hand, with 'Lambert Kt. of ye Golden Tulip' beneath.
He had withdrawn into what was then the country from political
life; but, amid his recreations as a florist, was doubtless watching
the opportunity for a return to the field of his professional work.
Next to Monk he was probably the most able of the generals of
the Commonwealth and Protectorate, and it was an error on
the part of Cromwell to have estranged him.

W. C. Hazlitt, *Gleanings in Old Garden Literature*, 1887

Frances Hodgson Burnett's most famous work is her children's classic The Secret Garden. *This excerpt describes exactly how a secret garden should be.*

from The Secret Garden

The sun was shining inside the four walls and the high arch of blue sky over this particular piece of Misselthwaite seemed even more brilliant and soft than it was over the moor. The robin flew down from his tree-top and hopped about or flew after her from one bush to another. He chirped a good deal and had a very busy air, as if he were showing her things. Everything was strange and silent and she seemed to be hundreds of miles away from any one, but somehow she did not feel lonely at all. All that troubled her was her wish that she knew whether all the roses were dead, or if perhaps some of them had lived and might put out leaves and buds as the weather got warmer. She did not want it to be a quite dead garden. If it were a quite alive garden, how wonderful it would be, and what thousands of roses would grow on every side! …

She went slowly and kept her eyes on the ground. She looked in the old border beds and among the grass, and after she had gone round, trying to miss nothing, she had found ever so many more sharp pale green points and she had become quite excited again.

'It isn't a quite dead garden,' she cried out softly to herself. 'Even if the roses are dead, there are other things alive.'

She did not know anything about gardening, but the grass seemed so thick in some of the places where the green points were pushing their way through they did not seem to have room enough to grow. She searched about until she found a rather sharp piece of wood and knelt down and dug and weeded out the weeds and grass until she made nice little clear places around them.

Frances Hodgson Burnett, *The Secret Garden,* 1909

The Cit's Country Box

Now bricklay'rs, carpenters and joiners,
With Chinese artists and designers
Produce their schemes of alteration
To work this wond'rous reformation.
The useful dome, which secret stood
Embosom'd in the yew-tree's wood,
The trav'ler with amazement sees
A temple, Gothic or Chinese,
With many a bell, and tawdry rag on
And crested with a sprawling dragon;
A wooden arch is bent astride
A ditch of water, four feet wide,
With angles, curves and zig-zag lines
From Halfpenny's exact designs.
In front, a level lawn is seen,
Without a shrub upon the green,
Where taste would want its first great law,
But for the skulking, sly ha-ha,
By whose miraculous assistance
You gain a prospect two fields distance.

Robert Lloyd, 1757

Elspeth Thompson is a friend, but one I never knew was a passionate gardener until I started reading her weekly column in The Sunday Telegraph. *I knew she knew all about the theory, because she worked on a gardening magazine. But, despite what readers think, those of us who pontificate to them may be less knowledgeable than we boast. In Elspeth's case, she put theory into practice with an allotment and started a steep learning curve. Here is her description of how it all started.*

The allotment

28 April 1996

It's a long time since I've been this tired and this dirty. I have not taken up mud wrestling (though to look at me two hours ago you might have thought I had), nor some other grubby hobby. No – I have just taken on an allotment. It happened quite suddenly, the way alarming new commitments sometimes do, but London allotments are like gold dust and previous vain attempts to secure one have taught me that you have to be on the ball. One minute I was at a party, chatting to my friend Sarah about her plot in the part of South London to which I'll be moving next month – she thought there might be one free. Next thing I knew I was down there myself, signing my agreement to a ferocious set of rules (plots to be kept cultivated and weed-free on pain of confiscation; pets under sufferance; visitors by strict permission only), and handing over the princely annual rent of £19.80 for – a pile of rubbish.

It was our own fault. I'd gone along with my boyfriend, Frank, who had nobly volunteered his considerable manpower for what I think he then considered another of my foolhardy schemes, and my sister, who for a share of the harvest had agreed to lend a hand with the heavy work and with watering in high summer. We were shown a perfectly good allotment that had recently become free and was in need only of a little light weeding. In the back of my mind I suppose it wasn't quite what I'd had in mind – no little shed, bordered by a busy road on one side and on the other three by intimidatingly professional-looking crops that made me and my *Organic Vegetables for Beginners* handbook suddenly feel shy and inadequate. But I was quite prepared to go for it until the man with the clipboard uttered the fateful words: 'There is another one I could show you, but you won't want it.' Says who?

Off we trekked across the little turf paths between embryonic onions and pubescent red rhubarb, past rickety cold frames and rusty water butts, until we reached the opposite corner of the site.

'That's it. Number 26,' he said, shaking his head.

The ground was uneven, and the few patches of soil visible under the mouldy red carpet, holey groundsheets and strewn plastic bottles were thick with couch grass and brambles. About a third of the plot seemed to have been used as a tip. But it was peaceful and private, away from the roar of the traffic, and bordered on the west side by a hawthorn hedge (imagine a little wooden bench there, to sit on in the shade on summer evenings), and, to the south, by a tall fence (can't you just see it strung with runner beans, sunflowers and morning glory?) More importantly, the soil, under all the carpet and debris (which even I knew would have kept down the worst of the weeds), was dark, soft, slightly crumbly and full of fat pink worms.

'Let's take it,' I said.

The next weekend we all turned up for action, feeling rather conspicuous with our shiny new spades. Twelve hours, two bonfires and a turf war with our neighbour later (all quite amicable, and we won), and two-thirds of the plot was roughly dug over and clear of rubbish and weeds. We left just as the sun was going down over the hedge, and in the low orange light the neat little plots with their bamboo stakes and skip-timber sheds had a kind of makeshift, shanty-town beauty. I know I am going to love this place.

Elspeth Thompson, *Urban Gardener,* 1999

Acknowledgments

Every effort has been made to contact copyright holders; in the event of an inadvertent omission or error, please notify the editorial department at Ryland Peters & Small, Kirkman House, 12–14 Whitfield Street, London W1T 2RP

Ryland Peters & Small wishes to thank the following writers, publishers and literary representatives for their permission to use copyright material:

Sue Bennett from *Five Centuries of Women and Gardens*, copyright © Sue Bennett 2000. Reproduced by kind permission of the National Portrait Gallery, London.

George Carter from 'The Shock of the Old', copyright © George Carter 2000. First published in *Country Life Gardens*.

Beth Chatto, 'Unusual Plants', copyright © Beth Chatto 1997. From the Beth Chatto Gardens and Nursery catalogue. Reproduced by kind permission of Beth Chatto.

Nigel Colborn from an article on Miriam Rothschild published in *Hortus*, vol. 9, spring 1990. Reproduced by kind permission of the editor of *Hortus*, Bryansground, Stapleton, Nr Presteigne, Herefordshire LD8 2LP (www. hortus.co.uk)

Robert Dash from 'English Bones, American Flesh', published in *Hortus*, vol. 4, winter 1987. Reproduced by kind permission of the editor of

Hortus, Bryansground, Stapleton, Nr Presteigne, Herefordshire LD8 2LP (www. hortus.co.uk).

Helen Dillon, 'Miss Wilmott' and 'The Yellow Garden' from *On Gardening* (TownHouse & CountryHouse, 1998). Reprinted with permission of TownHouse & CountryHouse Ltd, Dublin.

The Economist extract, copyright © The Economist Newspaper Ltd, London, 1992, from its issue of 12 July 1992.

Robert Frost, 'Rose Pogonias' from *The Poetry of Robert Frost* edited by Edward Connery Lathem, The Estate of Robert Frost and Jonathan Cape as publisher; copyright 1934, © 1969 by Henry Holt & Co., copyright © 1962 by Robert Frost. Used by permission of the Random House Group Ltd and Henry Holt & Company LLC, New York.

Leslie Geddes-Brown, 'But Robin insisted … ', copyright © Leslie Geddes-Brown 1987. First published in *The World of Interiors*, January 1987.

Geoffrey Grigson from *The Englishman's Flora* (Phoenix House, 1958). Reproduced by permission of the Orion Publishing Group, London.

David Hicks from *My Kind of Garden* (The Garden Art Press, an imprint of the Antique Collectors' Club, Woodbridge, 1999). Reproduced by permission of the Antique Collectors' Club Ltd.

Penelope Hobhouse from *Garden Style* (Frances Lincoln, 1988), copyright © Penelope Hobhouse 1988. Reproduced by permission of Frances Lincoln Ltd, 4 Torriano Mews, Torriano Avenue, London NW5 2RZ.

Robin Lane Fox from *Better Gardening* (R & L, 1982), copyright © Robin Lane Fox 1982.

Christopher Lloyd from *Garden Flowers* (Cassell, 2000), copyright © Christopher Lloyd 2000. Reproduced by permission of the Orion Publishing Group, London.

Christopher Lloyd from *The Well-Tempered Garden* (Collins, 1970), copyright © Christopher Lloyd 1970. Reproduced by permission of HarperCollins Publishers Ltd and the author.

Michael Loftus, 'Pelargoniums' and 'Auriculas' from *The Plantsman's Handbook 2001*, copyright © Michael Loftus 2001. Reproduced by kind permission of the author.

Mirabel Osler, 'Why Garden?', published in *Hortus*, vol. 5, spring 1988. Reproduced by kind permission of the editor of *Hortus*, Bryansground, Stapleton, Nr Presteigne, Herefordshire LD8 2LP (www. hortus.co.uk).

Anna Pavord from *The Tulip* (Bloomsbury, 1999).

Roger Phillips and Leslie Land from *The 3,000 Mile Garden: an Exchange of Letters Between Two Eccentric Gardeners* (Pan, 1992), copyright © Roger Phillips and Leslie Land 1992.

John Raven from *A Botanist's Garden* (Collins, 1971). Reproduced by kind permission of Faith Raven.

Miriam Rothschild, Kate Garton, Lionel de Rothschild, from *The Rothschild Gardens* (Gaia, 1996).

Vita Sackville-West from 'The White Garden' from *In Your Garden* (Michael Joseph, 1951), copyright © Vita Sackville-West 1951. Reproduced with permission of Curtis Brown Group Ltd on behalf of the Estate of Vita Sackville-West.

Vita Sackville-West from 'Metasequoia' and 'Small Leaved Roses' from *In Your Garden Again* (Michael Joseph, 1953), copyright © Vita Sackville-West 1953. Reproduced with permission of Curtis Brown Group Ltd on behalf of the Estate of Vita Sackville-West.

Anne Scott-James from *Gardening Letters to My Daughter* (Michael Joseph, 1990), copyright © Anne Scott-James 1990.

Osbert Sitwell from *Left Hand, Right Hand* (Macmillan, 1945), copyright © Osbert Sitwell 1945. Reproduced by permission of the Estate of Osbert Sitwell.

Elspeth Thompson from 'The Allotment' from *Urban Gardener* (Orion, 1999), copyright © Elspeth Thompson 1999.

Edith Wharton from 'Villa Gamberaia' from *Italian Villas and Their Gardens* (The Century Company, 1903). Reprinted by permission of the Estate of Edith Wharton and the Watkins/Loomis Agency.

Picture credits

Illustrations by Helen Smythe, Polly Raynes, Sarah Kensington, Amanda Patton, David Ashby, Ann Winterbotham, Gill Tomblin and Lesley Craig.

Line drawings reproduced from *Plants & Flowers* courtesy of Dover Publications, Inc., New York.

ph = photographer

page 2 ph Pia Tryde; **6 ph** Pia Tryde/garden of Vanessa de Lisle, Fashion Consultant, London; **8 ph** Melanie Eclare/Marc Schoellen's garden, 'La Bergerie' in Luxembourg (+352 327 269); **12 ph** Caroline Hughes; **16 ph** Melanie Eclare/Mirabel Osler's garden in Ludlow, Shropshire; **21 ph** Melanie Eclare/Jim Reynolds' garden 'Butterstream', Co. Meath, Ireland; **24 ph** Andrea Jones; **26 ph** Jan Baldwin; **27 ph** Andrea Jones; **28** Melanie Eclare/Fovant Hut Garden near Salisbury in Wiltshire was created by garden designer Christina Oates together with her husband Nigel and is open to the public (01722 714756); **31 ph** Pia Tryde; **33 ph** Andrea Jones; **34 ph** Caroline Hughes; **36 ph** Melanie Eclare/Marc Schoellen's garden, 'La Bergerie' in Luxembourg (+352 327 269); **38 ph** Melanie Eclare/garden of interior designer Suzanne Rheinstein, designed by Judy M. Horton (+1 323 462 1412); **44 ph** Melanie Eclare/Mirabel Osler's garden in Ludlow, Shropshire; **47 ph** Polly Wreford; **51 ph** © Jonathan Buckley; **52 ph** Melanie Eclare/Sticky Wicket wildlife garden near Dorchester, designed and

created by Peter and Pam Lewis (01300 345 476); **55 ph** Andrea
Jones; **57 ph** Melanie Eclare/Bryan's Ground, David Wheeler and
Simon Dorrell's garden in Herefordshire (01544 260001); **60 ph**
Melanie Eclare/garden designed by Judy Kameon–Elysian
Landscapes (+1 323 226 9588); **62 ph** Melanie Eclare/Jim Reynolds'
garden 'Butterstream', Co. Meath, Ireland; **65 ph** Melanie Eclare;
66 ph Christopher Drake/La Bastide Rose, Nicole & Pierre
Salinger's house, Le Thor, Provence; **68 ph** Melanie Eclare/
a garden in south London designed by Roberto Silva
(020 7700 7484); **74 ph** Melanie Eclare; **77 ph** Jerry Harpur;
78 ph Francesca Yorke; **91 ph** Caroline Hughes; **93 ph** Melanie
Eclare; **95 ph** Melanie Eclare; **100 ph** Caroline Hughes; **103 ph**
Andrea Jones; **105 ph** Jan Baldwin/interior designer Philip
Hooper's own house in East Sussex (020 7978 6662); **107 ph**
Andrea Jones; **108 ph** Tom Leighton; **110 ph** Caroline Hughes;
114 ph Andrea Jones; **117 ph** Caroline Hughes; **119 ph** Tom
Leighton; **120 ph** Pia Tryde/shed in the allotment garden of John
Matheson; **125 ph** Andrea Jones; **127 ph** Melanie Eclare; **129 ph**
Melanie Eclare/Mirabel Osler's garden in Ludlow, Shropshire;
134 ph Melanie Eclare/Sticky Wicket wildlife garden near
Dorchester, designed and created by Peter and Pam Lewis
(01300 345 476); **137 ph** Chris Tubbs; **139 ph** Andrea Jones;
140 ph © Steve Painter; **143 ph** Melanie Eclare/Farrell Family
garden, Woodnewton; **145 ph** Jan Baldwin; **151 ph** Melanie
Eclare/Sticky Wicket wildlife garden near Dorchester, designed and
created by Peter and Pam Lewis (01300 345 476); **152 ph** Melanie
Eclare/a garden in south London designed by Roberto Silva
(020 7700 7484); **155 ph** © Jonathan Buckley.

Index of authors

A
Aubrey, John 61

B
Bacon, Francis 22–3
Beckford, William 65
Bennett, Sue 131–3
Bonaparte, Napoleon 123
Bridges, Robert 78
Brooke, Rupert 20
Browne, William 90
Bryant, William Cullen 33
Burnett, Frances Hodgson 150–1
Burns, Robert 144

C
Carter, George 70–3
Chambers, William 69
Chatto, Beth 54–5
Clare, John 45
Colborn, Nigel 137
Cowper, William 115, 143

D
Dash, Robert 26–7, 130
Defoe, Daniel 56
Dillon, Helen 30–2, 124–6

E
Earle, Mrs C. W. 118
Eliot, George 35
Ellacombe, Canon H. N. 119
Ely, Helen Rutherford 140
Emerson, Ralph Waldo 101, 107

F
Falkner, John Meade 24
Farrer, Reginald 85–9
Frost, Robert 53
Fuller, Thomas 77

G
Geddes-Brown, Leslie 63–4, 141–2
Gissing, T. W. 117
Grigson, Geoffrey 93–4

H
Hazlitt, W. Carew 149
Hentzner, Paul 50
Herbert, George 16
Hicks, David 42–3, 127–8
Hobhouse, Penelope 59–60
Hooker, Joseph 92
Howell, James 51

J
Jekyll, Gertrude 34, 79
Johns, Rev C. A. 111–12

L
Land, Leslie 109–10
Lane Fox, Robin 104–5
Leigh, Dr C. 58
Lloyd, Christopher 102–3, 146–7
Lloyd, Robert 152
Loftus, Michael 96–7, 106

M
Marvell, Andrew 100
Merritt, Anna Lea 148
More, Thomas 19

N
Nevill, Dorothy 92
North, Marianne 25–6, 112–13, 138–9

O
Osler, Mirabel 10–15

P
Pavord, Anna 76–7
Pepys, Samuel 62
Phillips, Roger 109–10

R
Raven, John 80–1
Rothschild, Miriam 135–6

S
Sackville-West, Vita 47–8, 82–4
Scott-James, Anne 17–18, 46
Shakespeare, William 95
Sitwell, Osbert 49–50, 122
Swinburne, Algernon Charles 37
Switzer, Stephen 116

T
Temple, William 67–8
Tennyson, Alfred, Lord 29
Thompson, Elspeth 153–5

W
Wharton, Edith 40–1